# Made in Mexico

Tradition, Tourism,
and Political Ferment in Oaxaca

Chris Goertzen

UNIVERSITY PRESS OF MISSISSIPPI/JACKSON

www.upress.state.ms.us

The University Press of Mississippi is a member
of the Association of American University Presses.

Illustrations courtesy of the author unless otherwise noted

First printing 2010
∞
Library of Congress Cataloging-in-Publication Data

Goertzen, Chris.
  Made in Mexico : tradition, tourism, and political ferment in Oaxaca / Chris Goertzen.
     p. cm.
  Includes bibliographical references and index.
  ISBN 978-1-60473-796-7 (cloth : alk. paper) — ISBN 978-1-60473-797-4 (ebook)  1.
Heritage tourism—Mexico—Oaxaca (State) 2.  Handicraft—Mexico—Oaxaca (State)
3.  Festivals—Mexico—Oaxaca (State) 4.  Oaxaca (Mexico : State)—Social conditions.
5.  Textile crafts—Economic aspects—Mexico—Case studies.  I. Title.
  G155.M6G64 2010
  338.4'7917274—dc22                                        2010008991

British Library Cataloging-in-Publication Data available

# Contents

Made in Mexico

# Preface

I wandered around the main city square of the southern Mexican city of Oaxaca on an evening in early July 2007. Many sights on this *zócalo* were ones I'd viewed for a few weeks every year or so for decades. Most of the buildings are a century or two (or more) old, and there has been little turnover in the restaurants, stores, and government offices that occupy them. In the middle of the zócalo still stood the bandstand that I'd seen sheltering brass bands and marimbas so many times in other years, and most of the landscaping seemed familiar. The people seemed familiar as types, even if many individuals were new to me, and although many must have been newcomers to the city. Working-class and rich mestizos (both locals and visitors), impoverished Indians, and a variety of international tourists interacted in customary ways.

Tourists are always there, in fact, because this metropolis of about half a million, situated at the confluence of three broad mountain valleys in southern Mexico, presents an attractive mix of colonial architecture and exotic ethnicity, as well as pleasant weather and affordable amenities. Craft stands in customary locations on the square, as well as stores filled with more crafts and signs advertising ethnically based cultural entertainment (especially miniature forms of the state's giant annual festival, the Guelaguetza), line the square to attract those tourists.

Members of the city's middle and upper classes do have their own exclusive haunts on the relatively affluent north side of the city, including a U.S.-style shopping mall and nightclubs and discotheques where cover charges act as class-demarcating barriers. Nevertheless the nice restaurants on and near the central zócalo remain both a festive family destination and a customary venue to publicly display these families' continued place at the pinnacle of Oaxaca's economy and power structure. Thus the local affluent were just as reliably represented as each of the square's other regular constituencies.

Just one aspect of zócalo demographics surprised me. During my two decades of intermittent observation, I'd always seen some evidence of social volatility in a small, clearly demarcated physical area, evidence of a simmering that was quite transparent and yet seemingly under control. That is, Indians from outside the capital have often camped along one edge of the square, the side with the government palace (so that their camp blocked no businesses, and the generous overhang of that long building protected their sleeping pallets from the rain). During several of my visits, one or another group of campers was in residence, quietly protesting the allegedly false imprisonment of much of the male leadership of their rural village. Something had gone wrong in their community that had resulted in violence followed by mass arrests, most likely an escalating agrarian dispute with a neighboring municipality. The wives and children of many of the imprisoned men, plus a few other relatives, now lived unhappily downtown, their misery in plain view of anyone who took a turn around the square. But such encampments were stable, their residents keeping protests within bounds in the usual circumscribed physical space and in an established etiquette, and were tolerated by the authorities.

This July, no such encampment was to be seen, and this absence was oddly disorienting. Instead, dozens of middle-class protesters had tables dispersed among the informal sales booths on the square. These protesters directed their anger not only toward the authorities but also toward the tourists whose financial infusions into Oaxaca were blamed for propping up the repellent status quo. This created a peculiar mosaic throughout this central public area, whereby many Oaxacans explicitly welcomed outsiders as potential customers while a significant minority just as clearly and publicly did not.

Most of the salespeople on the square represented families that make crafts for a living, crafts designed to please tourists (for examples of these products, see figures 1 and 2). Their goals are not in any grand political arena but are instead immediate and intimate—that is, to bring home enough money for dinner and shelter, and to do so day after day. Through an ever-evolving, informal, yet meticulous analysis of tourists' aesthetic and philosophical inclinations, the craftspeople and salespeople try to find common ground between what their family members can make and what the visitors will buy. The amount they earn seldom exceeds a pittance, but it doesn't take much to beat local daily wages. These families and their activities present a fascinating composite story, with paths of interaction between locals and tourists evident not just in conversation and in money changing hands but also in the nature of the artifacts and festivals they create. These objects and events must please both makers and purchasers for tourism to be sustainable in both socio-economic and psychological terms.

At the same time that most of these salespeople, like most of the citizens of the city of Oaxaca and environs, find being friendly to outsiders a natural product of enlightened self-interest, the protesters work at cross-purposes with that hospitable majority. They do work hard and, lately, with an effectiveness out of proportion with their numbers. Their banners and their spoken rhetoric make clear that they want tourists to go away, since much or most of the money generated by tourism supports a social order the protesters ardently wish to overturn. It is not new for the square to offer a visual juxtaposition of many poor people looking pleasant doing their jobs earning money serving affluent visitors while other citizens assert that the local power structure is acting badly on a grand scale. But what I saw in 2007 illustrated a new development, that the explicitly unhappy part of the cultural collage had literally gotten out of the box, escaped from one defined rectangle on the square to a peppering of smaller locations, no longer as easy for tourists to skirt, ignore, or consider as piquant punctuation of quaint sights.

Oaxaca has long attracted authors because of its rich history—evinced especially in spectacular ruins—and its even richer present, notably the cornucopia of indigenous ethnic cultures bubbling into the views of both tourists and academics through festivals and crafts. The state is home to forms of most of the types of crafts produced in Mexico, but Oaxaca is known especially for handwoven rugs and hand-carved and hand-painted wooden figures (called *alebrijes*). The rugs and figures have inspired a few attractive, semischolarly coffee table books, aimed at folk art enthusiasts and collectors. All these books are direct products of the interaction of tourism and tradition in Oaxaca, and all feature the combination of information and celebration typical of good guidebooks.

Figure 1. Two rugs woven in Teotitlán del Valle by the sons of Felipe Hernández. Inexpensive, small rugs (about 14" x 20") offer a training opportunity for young weavers; their inevitable inconsistencies in technique do not add up to dramatically visible errors within such limited physical space. These two rugs contrast in general brightness, reflecting what Felipe believed were changes in customer taste between 1994 (pastel rug) and 1998 (brighter rug).

Figure 2. Animals carved from copal wood and elaborately decorated (with house paint), made in the late 1990s in San Martín Tilcajete by María Jiménez Ojeda and her siblings. The brothers carve, and all paint (to María's patterns, since she is the best-known artist in the family).

Figure 3. The Danza de la Pluma, the most famous and spectacular of the dances making up the giant festival called the Guelaguetza, on this occasion performed on the square in Oaxaca city in support of a protest (lasting several years) advocating the release of numerous political prisoners from the village of Loxicha.

Figure 4. The Loxicha protest encampment on the Oaxaca city square, late December 1999. Children painted the colorful banner seen here.

The best of these specialized books I have encountered as of this writing (in 2008), starting with the most thorough, include Andra Fischgrund Stanton's *Zapotec Weavers of Teotitlán* (1999, with photography by Jaye R. Phillips), an especially effective wedding of lovely pictures and informative prose; Shepard Barbash's *Oaxacan Woodcarving: The Magic in the Trees* (1993, with photography by Vicki Ragan); Arden Aibel Rothstein and Anya Leah Rothstein's *Mexican Folk Art from Oaxacan Artist Families* (2002), which concerns many types of Oaxacan crafts and contains sections on rugs, alebrijes, and black pottery; and John M. Forcey's *The Colors of Casa Cruz: An Intimate Look at the Art and Skill of Fidel Cruz, Award Winning Textile Weaver* (1999). All but Forcey's book are printed in color throughout, and all make their impact at least as much through excellent photographs as through prose. There is just one similar book on local festivals, Mary Jane Gagnier de Mendoza's beautiful and eloquently written *Oaxaca Celebration: Family, Food, and Fiestas in Teotitlán* (2005). State-sponsored videos for sale in museums, in tourist-oriented stores, and on eBay document each annual recurrence of Oaxaca's massive festival, the Guelaguetza.

In a parallel stream, there are many fine books on politics in Oaxaca. My favorites—if that is a suitable word given the gravity of the subject—are those by Arthur Murphy and Alex Stepick (*Social Inequality in Oaxaca: A History of Resistance and Change*, 1991) and Lynn Stephen (several books, most recently *Zapotec Women: Gender, Class, and Ethnicity in Globalized Oaxaca*, 2005). A few meticulous studies try to bridge the worlds of crafts and politics, the most recent being Michael Chibnik's *Crafting Tradition: The Making and Marketing of Oaxacan Wood Carvings* (2003) and W. Warner Wood's *Made in Mexico: Zapotec Weavers and the Global Ethnic Art Market* (2008). The present book is most closely allied to those. It is my own attempt to negotiate a pair of simultaneous equilibriums, one between politics broadly understood and ethnicity as expressed in crafts and festivals aimed at tourists, the other a matter of presentation, trying for the happy marriage achieved by Stanton and by Gagnier de Mendoza between prose and photography (I've balanced each thousand words with a picture).

I introduce the basic concepts threading through the book with a case study of a handwoven pillowcase from Chiapas, in the mountainous south of Mexico. The following two chapters widen the lens to the crafts and the central festival of Oaxaca, a state neither quite as far south nor as mountainous, and one with similar problems, which, however, are less susceptible to concise analysis. In the fourth chapter, I discuss crafts and associated culture flourishing outside the tourist-oriented economic and thus artistic gravitational fields (especially in Oaxaca, but with significant reference to Chiapas and to the Yucatán Peninsula). I close with what has to be a somber appraisal of recent events in Oaxaca, developments in which politics and tourism-supported ethnic arts have lost their long-term symbiosis and are very much at odds.

I am grateful to my wife Valerie and my daughters Kate and Ellen for traveling with me to Oaxaca several times and to Mérida once, and for putting up with my mix of work and play during what were unalloyed vacations for them. My former student and current friend Dolores Saenz checked my translations at various stages; I would have been much more clumsy without her cheerful and selfless aid. My thanks to the University of Southern Mississippi for the sabbatical during which I drafted the book; to Andra F. Stanton, Terry Zug, Dale Olsen, and Valerie Goertzen for reading late drafts of it; and to Craig Gill and the staff of the University Press of Mississippi for putting up with my highly idiosyncratic wishes once again. Above all, I thank the craftspeople, dancers, musicians, and merchants of Oaxaca, whose courtesy knows no bounds.

Made in Mexico

Figure 5. A pillowcase purchased in San Cristóbal, Chiapas, in 1997, in use in the author's home. A woman living in nearby San Andrés Larrainzar wove the central panel on a backstrap loom; a man wove the background cloth (likely in San Cristóbal itself) on a pedal loom.

# 1.

# Introductory Case Study:
# Tales Told by a Pillowcase from Chiapas

A beautiful pillow rests on a chair in our home in Louisiana. I bought the pillow's colorful cover in May 1997, in the far south of Mexico, in San Cristóbal de las Casas, the only sizable city in the highlands of Chiapas. My trip to the highlands was partly a happy accident. Air fares to Cancún were absurdly cheap that summer, so I flew there, then bussed to Mérida and San Cristóbal in turn, looking for crafts and events that would aptly complement those I encountered on numerous trips to my main research destination of Oaxaca. I would revisit Mérida and San Cristóbal later to further contextualize my experience in Oaxaca, but on this early, serendipitous trip, I already found much of interest.

I took photographs of the pillowcase as part of the research for this book. Later I returned to the store and reexamined the case with a tourist's eye. It was well crafted and reasonably priced, featured colors that drew in but did not jar the eye, bore a region-specific and striking pattern that later could evoke memories of the trip, and would pack easily—all characteristics of the perfect souvenir. It came home with me.

Later that year, I read accounts of a massacre perpetrated by paramilitary gunmen in Acteal, a hamlet within the municipality of Chenalhó—just thirty-seven kilometers into the mountains from San Cristóbal. Forty-five men, women, and children were slaughtered over a period of several hours. The victims were sympathetic to—or at least not hostile to—the antigovernment Zapatistas. Precisely how involved the archconservative local authorities were in the attack may never be known, though it is clear that the paramilitary group was financed and

3

trained by the PRI, the ruling party (Nash 2003, xiv), and that state police stationed in hearing distance of the gunshots did nothing to stop the
slaughter (Kovic and Eber 2003, 12).

Had the killers' trucks traveled just a few minutes in a different direction, they would have entered San Andrés Larrainzar, the *municipio* that
is home to the weaver of the central panel of my pillowcase. I could not
escape the thought that the elegant traditional craftsmanship embodied
in that object, the tourism that sponsored its creation, and the wanton
violence of this atrocity might well all express the working of the same
intertwined factors.

Might something similar happen in Oaxaca? Probably not, was my
first reaction. After all, the relationship between Indian countryside and
mestizo city seemed less strained in Oaxaca. But as I continued to read
about Chiapas and as I made more trips to Oaxaca, I began to wonder if differences between Mexico's two poorest states, the ones with
the greatest populations of Indians, might be less matters of principle
than of degree, and thus of the timing of dramatic events punctuating
longtime tensions: *when* rather than *if* violent unrest would occur. But
since both the exoticism of the attractions of ethnic tourism and the
symptoms of long-term socioeconomic tensions were more extreme in
Chiapas, the interaction of these forces was more starkly drawn there
through the 1990s. A look at the inevitable, uncomfortable intimacy between what draws outsiders to Indian Mexico and what shocks those
same outsiders will serve to introduce the themes of this book.

### Politics and Tradition in the History of Highland Chiapas

Chiapas has always been Mexico's least accessible state. Though arguably the richest in natural resources, it contains the largest populations
of the desperately poor and illiterate (Fábregas Puig and García 1994,
42). For example, Chiapas is the source of over half of Mexico's hydro-
electric power, but over half of the state lacks electricity (Collier 1994,
16). Highland Chiapas, together with the Yucatán Peninsula, neighboring Guatemala, and Belize, is home to about three million descendants
of the Maya Indians. As is true in all Indian areas of Central America, principal cities are Ladino (roughly synonymous with *mestizo*—of

mixed European and Indian blood—but Ladino also includes geneti-
cally pure Indians who have moved to the city and adopted mestizo culture). Surrounding villages include some Ladino merchants and more
Indians, and the countryside is completely Indian. This is true in much
of Oaxaca as well.

Highland Chiapas is stunningly beautiful. Mountains rise to over
nine thousand feet, and valleys such as the one cradling San Cristóbal
are around seven thousand feet. The elevation yields a temperate climate enticing to visitors, but the vistas and climate are not the primary
attractions: rather, it is the Indians, whom outsiders perceive as embodying an ancient and intriguing way of life, in addition to being cre-
ators of handsome crafts reflecting that timeless way of life. In fact, the
"authenticity" of modern Maya life—real or mythical—is not entirely
voluntary. The characteristics that anthropologists and tourists find so
fascinating resonate with a colonial and modern history unsurpassed
in Mexico in terms of the ill-treatment of Indians, and consequently of
friction between the few Ladinos in power and the many Indians forced
to endure a parade of humiliations.

Spaniards arrived in upland Chiapas in 1524 and founded San Cristóbal four years later. The colonial era here—as throughout Mexico—
saw Indians decimated by imported diseases, further ground down by
forced labor and taxes, and robbed of most of their arable land. But
while most of Mexico has experienced some political liberalization and
land reform, changes that might reduce the Ladino owners' power have
been vigorously and cunningly resisted here. Further, the meager economic benefits of the minimal reforms that have slipped past the ob-
duracy of the rich have been more than offset by population growth:
between 1950 and 1990, the population of the state more than tripled,
despite massive out-migration. When the right-wing dictator Porfirio
Díaz moved the state capital from San Cristóbal to the lowland city of
Tuxtla Gutiérrez in 1891, it was because he considered San Cristóbal to
be too conservative. Friction has bubbled into open conflict regularly
here, notably in the rebellions of the 1530s, an uprising in the 1780s inspired by a religious vision, the so-called caste wars of the late 1860s,
unrest linked to bootlegging in the late 1950s,[1] and the Zapatista uprising that commenced in 1994. What is most unusual about the recent

unrest is that it attracted the attention of the press, and this publicity pressured Mexico's central government to intervene.

Today San Cristóbal is a town of about a hundred thousand Ladinos (and a few thousand Indians in slums) surrounded by over a million other Indians. In earlier times, life in the highlands revolved around seasonal subsistence agriculture alternating with labor in the lowlands, a strategy that can no longer sustain booming populations. Authority in the villages remains vested in a complex system that is both religious and civil. Men raise their standing in the community by assuming expensive religious obligations in what anthropologists call a cargo system. For instance, one man might pay for flowers for a year's heavy calendar of festivals, another might sponsor fireworks, another could pay for musicians' strings, and so on. The system thus substitutes enhancements in prestige for economic betterment: it promotes financial leveling.

Outlying villages like Chamula and Zinacantan fit classic definitions of peasant life: culture is inward looking and carefully circumscribed, social life is intense and largely egalitarian, and religion is critical in the social control of wealth. Nevertheless, the sense of community in even these intensely conservative highland villages is clearly on the wane (see Cancian 1992, 201). It is tempting to believe that this traditional culture came under siege only recently, but that assertion would not merely be false but would obscure a critical factor in the formation of the threatened culture. It is likely that the religion-centered skein of local identities and associated expressive culture—including crafts—has intensified over many centuries as a cumulative defensive reaction to threats to this culture. To become sympathetic to this interpretation, we must shelve romantic views of this tradition as, in the words of Frank Collier, "vestigial or residual [in favor of seeing it] as constituting a dynamic response that Indians make to their peripheral position in a larger, changing system" (1975, 15, following Aguirre Beltran 1967/1979). Indeed, the villages nearest to San Cristóbal, which one might expect to be the most assimilated owing to their proximity to city life, actually remain the most adamantly distinctive.

Tourists constitute the third wave of outsiders to invade highland Chiapas during the twentieth century. The first wave of intruders, initially a trickle but cumulatively powerful in effect, was Protestant missionaries. When the second wave, anthropologists, arrived in substantial numbers in the 1950s, they found that one of their first important tasks was to demonstrate that they were not yet another beachhead of evangelists. Evon Z. Vogt, the distinguished leader of the Harvard Chiapas Project, found that he and his colleagues had to overcome Indians' initial wariness by smoking and drinking publicly (1994, 103). Perhaps the barriers that scholars had to penetrate before being permitted to study modern Maya religion had been exacerbated by missionary activity. After all, when Protestants advocated abandoning the local religious festival system—an argument with immediate economic appeal, since festival support was so expensive—they were fomenting the overturning of all authority, since religious and civil authority were and always have been thoroughly intertwined.[2]

Tourism was slow to arrive in San Cristóbal. Guidebooks about Mexico published before World War II almost never mention Chiapas or even Oaxaca (e.g., Franck and Lanks 1942; Garner 1937; Gilpatrick 1911; Goolsby 1936; and Jackson 1937). In 1938, Graham Greene did make a point of traveling to San Cristóbal but found it a challenging destination. The mountains of Chiapas seemed "like a prison wall" that he conquered only by undertaking what proved to be a "hellish mule ride" (1939, 153, 168). Although the Pan-American Highway arrived in 1946 and was paved in 1950, sheer distance continued to impede the flow of travelers. Tourism would not boom until well into the 1970s with the growth of air travel. Today about three-fourths of all visitors are Europeans who fly to Tuxtla Gutiérrez, then bus to San Cristóbal.

Some approaches to being a tourist feature reduced mental activity and responsibility through emphasizing physical pleasure, thus justifying Aldous Huxley's assertion that "we read and travel not that we may broaden our minds, but that we may pleasantly forget they exist" (1925, 12). Conversely, Dean MacCannell described "sightseeing" as "a kind of collective striving for a transcendence of the modern totality, a way of attempting to overcome the discontinuity of modernity, of incorporating its fragments into unified experience" (1975, 13). There is a flavor of a pilgrimage here, which Graburn made more explicit. He noted that "holiday" formerly meant "holy day," when much of a year's travel would be spent going to religious festivals. Other types of journeys have largely replaced the literal pilgrimage over time, but some of the ritual and the hunt for life's deeper meanings remain (1989, 26). Glassie put it simply: "Tourists today include pilgrims, people serious on their journey" (1993, 322). Of course, today's tourist-pilgrims vary in how much intelligence and industry they can or care to muster. Also, and of critical importance, the quest that MacCannell and Graburn describe is often—perhaps usually—mixed in individual tourists with the "switching-off" that topped a survey conducted by Krippendorf of German tourists' motives for travel (1987, 23). Cohen put his conclusions more diplomatically: while some tourists are discriminating (his higher-toned categories are "experimental" and "experiential"), "recreational tourists, who seek in the Other mainly enjoyable restoration and recuperation and hence tend to approach the cultural products encountered on their trip with a playful attitude of make believe, will entertain much broader criteria of authenticity" (1988, 2).

Tourists who journey to San Cristóbal can easily indulge in some "switching off," since the city is a beautiful location with a relaxing climate and a well-developed infrastructure of hotels and service employees. But most tourists, whether carrying backpacks or Italian leather luggage, *do* incorporate into their visits some measure of a romantic quest to view an embodiment of an earlier, presumably better—and to them certainly more exotic—way of life. My experience with this tourist population, one to which I belong on some days, is that its members are intellectually active and curious about indigenous culture during their visits, mean well in a general way, and certainly don't want to hurt the culture on which their holiday is based (I would call them/us "ethnic" tourists or perhaps "romantic ethnic" tourists). But to the Indians, the sheer affluence of these visitors is disturbing: the contrast between the standards of living of visitor and visited is incomprehensible and cannot but inspire envy and suspicion.

Throughout history, wealthy landowners took the Indians' property and sometimes their very lives. But the oppressors despised or ignored Indian culture, which therefore remained the Indians' own, and a locus of spiritual refuge. When the Indians finally began to accept money to let tourists learn about their religion, and when they began to sell crafts that seemed to bear deep cultural significance, was a soul-robbing tragedy taking place? Not completely. Such commoditization has often been said to "destroy the authenticity of local cultural products and human relations," but how this works out in individual cases can be quite nuanced (Cohen 2004, 101). For instance, tourists are prevented from delving too deeply into religion in the highlands by the frequent prohibition of photography, the rationing of entrance into churches, and the barrier of language; it is a rare tourist who can tune into prayers spoken in Tzotzil or any other modern Maya language.

I will concentrate here on what we can learn about the maintenance of, and changes in, traditional life from how craft items are designed, made, and sold.

### One Pillowcase as a Site of Negotiation between Tourism and Tradition

Craftspersons who sell their creations *may* be allowed to express tradition in the best ways they know how, but *must* make things that fit or can shape the expectations of their customers. Thus the Indians who market hard-won skills and enduring symbols know that the arbiters of the effectiveness of their efforts are their customers. It is nearly impossible to have a conversation with a craftsperson that escapes this commercial shadow, and perhaps it is willful and unseemly to insist on chatting about aesthetics and techniques when the wolf is so near to many of their doors. Nevertheless each craft object represents a negotiation in which artisans' and customers' images of authenticity (and of beauty) match, conflict, or can be reconciled. Craftspersons may have to bend a little (or a lot), although their customers might prefer to believe that no such yielding takes place. As McKean noted, it is "especially in the performing and plastic arts" that "tourists expect the perpetuation of ancient traditions" (1989, 126). The ideal craft object is arguably authentic, artfully balances the understandable and the palatably mysterious, and, of course, is visually attractive to both maker and customer.

Although many tourists in highland Chiapas base their purchases on perceived authenticity, they generally lack detailed knowledge to inform their judgments. In fact, while both Indian craftspersons and tourists harbor complex notions about what is important in tradition, neither population can easily articulate those notions. I believe that the best window on the negotiation of authenticity as embodied in the craft object is the testimony of the object itself. In this introductory case study, the witness at hand is a pillow cover, an untraditional object handwoven in traditional ways, one presenting a modern version of an ancient and sacred design, an object made with the tourist in mind. Should we consider its existence a symptom of another layer of colonization, in which the craftsperson must debase his or her work and values to earn a living? Or is it a natural and healthy outgrowth of tradition?

We can approach answers to these questions by carefully reading the details of this "text," the pillowcase. This reading reveals a series of artistic decisions that stake out common ground between craftsperson and customer, decisions that are guided by an intermediary, the director of textiles for a cottage industry. At the same time, we see departures from tradition that follow familiar paths within the process of folkloric intensification (an umbrella term I will employ for the accruing of visual impact—through a fascinating variety of means—that generally takes place when craft tilts toward art). I analyze the following factors: (1) the fact that a sacred design decorates this pillow case, (2) the identity of the design, (3) the size of this version of the design, (4) the number and choice of colors used, (5) techniques of weaving, and (6) the process by which this item was designed and marketed.

### Sacred Designs on an Ornamental Pillowcase

Patterns such as the one on my pillowcase have as their primary home *huipiles*, elaborately handwoven blouses that bear a carefully ordered series of sacred designs. The huipiles themselves have become important as cultural symbols. But a pillowcase fits into the broad category of samplers, pieces of cloth on which weavers explore the effects of various combinations of patterns and of colors without devoting nearly as much time as is needed to finish a huipil. Moreover, sacred patterns on samplers can escape the weight of tradition and the narrative logic that governs their use on huipiles. Samplers may end up as small tablecloths, panels of purses, and so on; a pillowcase is a plausible use for a sampler.

Figure 6. A close-up of the "ancestors" pattern woven on the central panel of the pillowcase.

*The Identity of This Design*

This particular sacred pattern is common in its home municipio, San Andrés Larrainzar. While some designs have up to four distinct meanings (Morris 1987, 116), this one corresponds to a single slightly elastic meaning, variously known as "man and woman," "father and mother," or, most commonly, "ancestors." The man's arms reach toward the heavens; the woman's curl toward earth. In many versions of the design, her arms appear in several pairs, with the lower sets representing cornstalks. In a photographic catalog of rugs at a government-sponsored store called La Albarrada, the following sentence accompanies the pattern: "Los antepasados que sobrevivieron el diluvio obedecieron a dios y sembraron maiz" (The ancestors who survived the deluge obeyed God and cultivated corn). A more extended narrative appears in a brochure distributed by the government-sponsored store Casa de Artesanias. The brochure gives the sentence quoted at La Albarrada, then proceeds: "The ancestors protect society and, through dreams, teach the proper way to live. They are supernatural beings like the saints" (*Programa Artesanal* n.d., 2).[3]

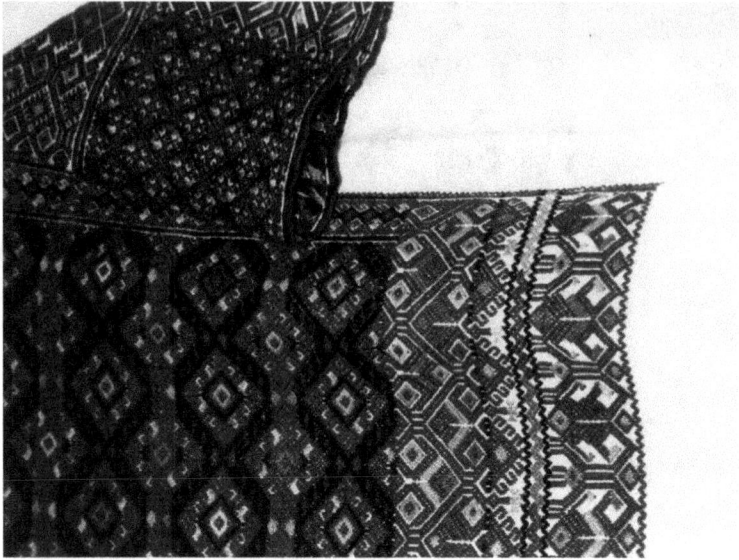

Figure 7. A huipil (traditional blouse) from San Andrés Larrainzar, for sale in San Cristóbal. While the ubiquitous diamond (universe) pattern dominates, other patterns also appear, notably "ancestors," employed, as it often is, as a border on the arm and body sections of the garment.

Just as both the title and narrative implications of this pattern exist in slight variations, so does the pattern itself. The model of the pattern kept in the mind of the Indian craftsperson is fluid, stored "in dreams," as they typically put it. When a pattern exists in many versions, the simpler versions of that pattern are the most sacred (Morris, in conversation, May 1997). The form on this pillowcase is near the complicated end of the spectrum of versions of "ancestors" and thus is suitable for use on a primarily decorative object.

When presented on a huipil, a row of "ancestors" is often used as a border, as on a contemporary huipil from San Andrés, one of many very similar—but never identical—huipiles for sale in the summer of 1997 in the San Andrés section of Sna Jolobil (see the section on cooperatives later in this chapter). Perhaps the fact that "ancestors" often reposes on a fabric's edge makes it especially easy to break off for a solo appearance. The design has an impeccable pedigree in tradition, but when it is used alone on an object such as my pillowcase, the visual effect is amplified and emphasized. Intensification through selection thus helps turn an authentic craft that had been as much aimed at the soul as at the eyes into satisfactory art for outsiders.

Another reason that "ancestors" is an apt design to appear singly is that it can be considered broadly representative of all the basic graphic approaches to shaping these designs. Morris places these design motifs in four categories: (1) diamonds representing earth and sky as a unity, (2) undulatory forms (e.g., snakes) representing earth, (3) "forms with three vertical lines which symbolize the foundation of the world, the community and its history," and (4) representational figures (1984, 11). That "ancestors" is representational helps at least some part of its message to translate easily; the pairing of a man and woman can nowhere seem meaningless. In addition, "ancestors" includes the ground graphic elements of diamonds, curves, and sets of three vertical lines in logical locations within the total design. Diamonds make up the man's head and the woman's, and more diamonds align vertically with their heads, marking their place in the universe. The lower pairs of limbs on the woman's body, which represent corn, curve: the corn issues from the earth. Last, since men have always dominated religion in Maya society, it is the male figure who reaches upward, who touches three vertical lines with each arm and with his head, and whose very body is composed of three vertical lines. In short, "ancestors" presented alone can substitute for a series of many patterns because it really is many patterns in one.

*The Size of This Version of the Design*

The design as worked out on my pillowcase is significantly larger than is common, especially on huipiles. Of course, this pattern never gets as small as the most diminutive patterns, such as the diamond (universe) pattern, because "ancestors" has many elements and contours, even in its simplest incarnations. Its large embodiment here pleases customers because the resultant impression is bold, actually hovering nicely between being pictorial and receding into an overall texture. And this size is not *too* out of line with tradition: this particular pattern is often made larger than neighboring patterns when it decorates the border of a huipil. Craftspersons for whom time is money welcome larger designs because they are faster to execute.

A certain fluidity in the shape and size of each design is built into tradition, since these craftspersons rarely work from sketches or any concrete plan but rather take their inspiration "from dreams," which do not include exact thread counts. Dreams partake of the supernatural and offer a sacred endorsement of what an outsider might call creativity. The guidance of dreams also helps the weaver to get around a potential practical difficulty: changing the size of a design by certain increments often entails adjustments in shape. This is because weaving, unlike painting, must obey mathematical logic: the weaver can make an image taller or wider by the thickness of three or four or five threads, but not by three and a half or four and a half. If, for instance, a design in one realization is one-third as wide as it is tall, and its height is increased by the thickness of two threads, a faithful maintaining of proportion would require widening it by two-thirds of a thread. The weaver must instead widen the pattern by one thread or not at all, either fattening the figure or narrowing it.

## The Number and Choice of Colors: Types of Intensification

That there are just three colors on the panel of the pillowcase is unusual from a historical perspective but does fit into one of a trio of modern trends. The general practice until recently was for crafts such as huipiles to employ most or all readily available colors. In a typical huipil from San Andrés, for example, the background was white or off-white, the dominant color set woven onto that field was red (or sometimes black), and perhaps a half-dozen other colors were added as accents.

At some point, the number of available colors exceeded the number that could reasonably be included on a given article, and self-conscious choice became a larger part of the process of selecting colors. Some modern craftspersons stick to densities of information typical of earlier decades. Indian weavers who sell through the prestigious cooperative Sna Jolobil frequently follow this "classical" approach. They hold to the letter of tradition—the earlier average number of colors and patterns—rather than the spirit, which was to exploit most or all of the available selection. These huipiles merit their daunting prices because of the high level of their craftsmanship, illustrating intensification through virtuosity. Other modern weavers make their patterns somewhat more dense and use more colors than employed in the past. The governing principle here is "the more the merrier"; in other words, "the more authentic details and colors, the more authentic the piece," or intensification through addition. This approach yields products that are real eye-catchers in many local boutiques but may seem garish back in Milwaukee.

The third general option is instead to pare down visual complexity by employing fewer colors and patterns than was typical historically. This choice offers a rationed fillip of the exotic while matching or complementing a customer's color scheme at home. Pillowcases like mine follow this model of carefully measured intensification through selection. It is important to note that each of these three avenues represents a historical rupture. The unselfconscious perpetuation of age-old tradition that many tourists prefer to believe that they are witnessing and purchasing and that most salesmen claim is in force is not an available option.

The picture is further complicated by the history of dyes used in the Chiapas highlands, a history with parallels elsewhere in Mexico. Craftspersons first used natural dyes. When synthetic dyes for wool and synthetically dyed ready-made cotton thread became available a few decades ago, natural dyes were rapidly abandoned. The new hues were brighter, more numerous, took less time to apply, and were more colorfast. The recent return to natural dyes (and to synthetic colors that look like those produced by natural dyes) resulted from outside intervention.

Ambar Past, an American, first came to Chiapas as a culture-oriented tourist in the early 1970s and later settled in San Andrés Larrainzar. She arrived eager to take up traditional weaving employing organic dyes, which she was dismayed to find had fallen out of use. She asked the local weavers about their grandmothers' dyeing techniques and soon was experimenting with old and new mordants (metallic compounds that combine with organic dyes to keep them from decomposing and fading). Originally working on her own time and nickel, she soon received support (support that an Indian would not have known how to seek) from various government organizations to study and eventually teach the use of these dyes. At first she had to pay her skeptical Indian associates to work with the natural tints, which they didn't like, as they found them relatively subdued and "sad." But their reluctance ebbed when they saw that tourists preferred articles thus dyed. By 1976, Indian women trained in the use of natural dyes by this outsider, who had synthesized some of these same women's memories of their ancestors' practices, had joined forces with the weavers and had begun teaching their techniques. Past could bow out, moving on to activities I will describe later in the chapter (conversation 1997).

Tourists' romantic enthusiasm for natural dyes refracted back into the municipio, and soon other villages were employing natural dyes in weavings for their own use as well as on garments for sale. This illustrates a process that McKean termed "cultural involution," in which a combination of economic necessity and social conservation brought crafts that had been made newly conservative for the sake of tourists back into local culture with that transformation intact (1989, 135). Today a new synthesis is under way, with natural and natural-looking dyes still dominating somewhat in practice and overwhelmingly in rhetoric—but with bright synthetic dyes used too, if sparingly. My pillowcase is of purchased cotton thread (more comfortable than homegrown wool) in colorfast synthetic colors approximating colors available in natural dyes.

White is the traditional background color for many types of highland weaving, and bright red a common accent, but the other color on my pillowcase, an extremely dark purple, has no historical precedent. Its effect is of an enlivened black. Of course, the broad impression of dark patterns bearing bright accents, all on a white field, is on target. The only surprise is that the traditional flat black is supplanted by an improved, vibrant version. I doubt that this bothered the weaver. The few colors work together beautifully, and the dark purple offers a complexity that makes up for the untraditional employment of so few separate colors.

## Techniques of Weaving

The pillowcase consists of a decorative panel woven on a backstrap loom by a woman; that panel is set into a larger piece of cloth woven on the colonial pedal loom, normally the province of men. Women can set up their backstrap looms almost anywhere. These small looms hang in the air, one end extending to a loop wrapped around the weaver's back—hence the equipment's name—and the other tied around a tree or to a nail. Women can use such looms as they mind children or sit in the market. There are limits to the size of cloth that can be made on a backstrap loom; larger pieces must be woven on the nonportable pedal loom, on which the sequence of thread crossings is more complex. The visual result of employing these two weaving techniques is that the texture of the cloth in the panel and that of the broader field contrast subtly and pleasingly.

The gendered division of labor that went into the creation of this pillowcase has parallels in textiles in Chiapas and parallels in tourist crafts throughout Mexico. The most direct precedent here is in the traditional assembly of women's outfits. Some women's outfits, for example, are made up of carefully decorated huipiles made on backstrap looms by women, and plain blue cloth skirts traditionally woven on pedal looms by men.

## Design and Marketing

Kun Kun, the store where I bought the pillowcase, is a fair-minded paternalistic enterprise, which, though run by highly educated outsiders, is operated with the primary goal of improving the welfare of Indians. Such cottage industries try to operate in a manner that respects tradition, and Kun Kun awards adequate (quite modest, but nonexploitative in local context) living wages to employees. The director of textiles, Maddalena Forcella (an Italian married to the store director, the Mexican anthropologist Luis Joel Morales), made many of the decisions I described in the previous sections about the pillowcase. In our discussions, she was not disposed to analyze her decisions as I have, but rather evinced an intuitive grasp of how to locate useful middle ground between her weavers and potential customers. In designing any object, she first selects an old pattern, feeling that customers prefer designs with explainable histories and that the craftspersons she employs may work more carefully with a design that they consider meaningful (though her own first criterion is that the design be attractive). I noticed that all the textiles in the store had a mixture of traditional and new colors roughly similar to those on my pillowcase but were always rendered in just one or two hues (perhaps over a white background).

Kun Kun supports about three hundred Indian shepherds, spinners, and weavers (most working in the municipios, but about twenty in production and sales on the premises in San Cristóbal). I asked who had made the pillow cover that I had purchased. Forcella said that the central panel was woven by a woman living in Bayalemó (a small hamlet fifteen minutes from the center of the municipio of San Andrés Larrainzar). The man who did the rest of the cloth worked on a pedal loom in the store in San Cristóbal. My sense was that all concerned in the manufacture and sale of this craft object were content with how things had been done, and that despite tremendous gulfs of various kinds between craftsperson and customer, this was a minimally stressful transaction in terms of aesthetics, identity, and money. But to what degree does this interaction represent others between Indian and tourist?

### Craft Outlets in San Cristóbal: Government and Private Stores

Tourists arriving in San Cristóbal immediately have opportunities to purchase crafts, and as they walk along the streets that join the main tourist destinations, visitors are never far from such opportunities. To picture San Cristóbal, imagine a lower-case letter *t* on which the right-hand (east) side of the crossbar extends twice as far as the left. The bus station is at the bottom (south end) of the t, where San Cristóbal's busiest street meets the Pan-American Highway. The tourist walking north toward the zócalo (the square, at the crossing of the t) passes restaurants, hotels, and plenty of souvenir shops. The best boutiques, along with many of the top hotels and restaurants, line up on the crossbar of the t, especially on its eastward extension. The main street above the square (the top of the t) passes the largest churches (near which stand the top textile cooperatives and the open-air craft market) on the way to the main market. And wherever the tourist walks, he or she will be hounded by hawkers carrying woven crafts.

Tourists want crafts to be both authentic—whatever that may mean to them—and attractive. Tourists' ability to interact with a craft object is determined by how much understanding they can muster, what prices they can pay, and what sizes they can transport. Craftspersons need remuneration for their work, access to the sales site (transportation, type, and location of shop), and prefer to work in a way that reinforces identity, allows some creativity, and maintains dignity. The abilities they bring to bear include craftsmanship (in the sense of learned skills); some combination of memory, research, and imagination; and ideally some modest capital, so they can take the time to make larger items or wait to be paid for finished crafts that are on consignment (rather than accepting the pittances paid by most middlemen).

*Cooperatives and Government-Sponsored Stores*

Textile cooperatives and government-sponsored stores offer the crafts that are the most "authentic," here meaning the closest to how items were made and looked a few generations ago—that is, within the modern era, but before the advent of mass tourism. Painstaking work means high prices, so sales locations must be central enough so that even the tourists with the least leisure, the Europeans whose package tours devote just a day or two to San Cristóbal, will enter these outlets. San Cristóbal's three main cooperatives are between the square and the market, within a block or so of the big churches. Sna Jolobil (Tzotzil for "Weavers' House") is the most successful of these cooperatives partly because it has the best location (Van Den Berghe 1994, 64–65; on the history of cooperatives in Chiapas, see Eber and Rosenbaum 1993).

Outlets share a critical element in their histories, the involvement of educated, altruistic intermediaries. The "best" transactions—that is, those most satisfactory in remuneration and mental comfort to the Indian craftsperson and in aesthetics and authenticity to customers—have been arranged through the cumulative diplomacy of culture brokers. Here Sna Jolobil again stands out. Walter F. "Chip" Morris, who now runs the most interesting museum-library-hotel in the city, Na Bolom, has long been the central scholar of modern Mayan textiles. During his earlier employment with FONART,[4] he had guided the formation of Sna Jolobil. Then he left it in the hands of a capable group of Indian women.

Such outlets market authenticity by displaying artifacts in ways referencing museums. The Casa de Artesanias, for example, has a side room containing a dozen dioramas illustrating life in specific municipios, several displays including statues of Indian women at backstrap looms. Few huipiles for sale match those in the museum alcove, but an implicit endorsement takes place: organizers inclined to mount a knowledgeable exhibition could certainly sell authentic textiles. Sna Jolobil follows a double "museum" strategy. The entire wall space is devoted to a series of sets of huipiles labeled by municipio. These and piles of similar garments stacked below the educational display are all for sale (at premium prices). One of the co-op managers works at her own backstrap loom just outside the entrance. Salespeople in such stores have been trained (first by the seminal middlemen, then by each other) not to be aggressive—as they are with one another in the market—but rather to wait patiently for customers to ask questions. Thus authentic-looking goods join museum-style exhibitions and outsider-style sales etiquette, an effective combination.

Such craft outlets usually focus on the local central craft of textiles in its most complex and traditional form, the huipil. However, samplers in the forms of pillowcases, napkins, and tablecloths are available for the customer who can't afford or wouldn't wear a huipil. Samplers don't seem out of place in huipil-dominated stores but become part of a visual sequence: the visitor sees Indian women with religious patterns on their blouses weaving on a backstrap loom just outside the doorway of the store, then similar garments bearing similar patterns for sale, then those patterns on other pieces of cloth useful to customers. Morris feels that Sna Jolobil has found its own style, basically "classical" (in conversation, 1997); he and the European customers (there are Americans, too, but not so many) have inspired a sort of insiders' nostalgic romanticism among the members of the co-op. Last, I would note again that the basic folkloric process of intensification is at work here, not in a crowding of effects within given items but through the visual impact of stunning craftsmanship and the juxtaposition of so many different beautiful garments.

*Paternalistic Cottage Industries Seeking New Market Niches*

This category of outlet overlaps considerably with the previous one: they share a type of middleman and, while privately operated, often get grants from the Mexican government or foreign foundations. Customers are discriminating but pursue the spirit rather than the letter of authenticity; tradition functions as an anchor for artistic play familiar to them from fashion in their home countries. Kun Kun, the source of my pillowcase, is such an outlet. The sampler textiles that constitute the second rung of offerings in the cooperatives here assume center stage and have been transformed as outlined in the discussion of my pillowcase.

Ambar Past, after stimulating the reintroduction of natural dyes in the highlands, settled down in San Cristóbal and founded the most adventurous of this category of outlets, Taller Leñateros. She speaks of her several dozen Indian and mestizo associates as "experimenting together." For instance, she paid Indian women to paint images from their dreams, which they had not done before, resulting in a wonderful book (1999).[5] Her atelier produces silk screens, woodcuts, handmade paper incorporating flowers, and a bilingual (Tzotzil-Spanish) manual on making and using natural dyes (1980). The attraction of these crafts is both aesthetic and historical—not in the sense of reproducing old things but rather in encompassing long-term change by juxtaposing ancient and modern motifs, such as on a T-shirt bearing a silk-screened illustration of a Maya god (pictured largely as in the ancient codices) happily astride a small motorcycle.

*Boutiques and Other Souvenir Stores*

These outlets, the most numerous type, range from elegant to shabby, with quality and price of wares highest near the town square. Most are run by Ladino businessmen whose main motivation is profit. They are not measurably more sympathetic to Indians than are local landowners. (A few owner-managers are American retirees with vaguely left politics who may be willing to accept lower profit margins than do most rapacious local entrepreneurs.) In most of these stores, the craftsperson faces the law of supply and demand, and since overpopulation dictates that the supply is always high, remuneration is reliably, humiliatingly low. This keeps prices in the better outlets below value too, since all stores compete for tourists' dollars. In addition, the owners of boutiques and souvenir stores have no particular commitment to *local* goods. These are emphasized because tourists often prefer the local imprimatur on authenticity and also because buying local items entails modest transportation costs and no additional layers of middlemen. Nevertheless a basic willingness to sell things from elsewhere has led many stores to feature not only local textiles but also, for instance, handblown glass from Guadalajara or carved animals from Oaxaca. There are also stores selling only silver jewelry from Taxco or local amber jewelry.

Although unalloyed authenticity is always a chimera, in these stores tradition is present much more in rhetoric than in fact. A few huipiles as historically accurate—and thus authentic in a literal sense—as those sold in Sna Jolobil hang beside endless arrays of cheaper ones decorated with varieties of flower patterns (sometimes older local designs, but often not). In the same stores, we also see garments of nontraditional types, such as full-length one-piece dresses decorated with traditional patterns crowded nearly beyond recognition, intensified to the point of caricature. Nevertheless even minimally authentic-looking products can incorporate forms of the processes that shape items like my pillowcase. The most typical decorations added to the gaudiest dresses as supplements to patterns like "ancestors" are of pictorial flowers and birds, which are traditional decorations in some highland communities, even if not the specific community that is the source of the basic pattern on the dress. And decorations placed on "new" parts of a garment are often linked in trails of ornament with embroidery in customary locations. Use of color can be analyzed similarly. But at some point decorations get too crowded, the chains of connections between tradition and innovation grow weak, and an article becomes even cheaper in appearance and meaning than in price.

Of course, boutiques do have important functions beyond the enrichment of Ladino businessmen. Many tourists who fly to Chiapas cannot extend their trips to the rest of Mexico and are grateful to have crafts from throughout the nation available in San Cristóbal. By the same token, craftspersons from elsewhere are happy to make sales far away from their own homes. And many of these crafts do express some sort of authenticity on the national rather than local level. Last, souvenir purchases of any kind can loosen the tourist's wallet, preparing them psychologically to buy more authentic and expensive goods.

## Indians Dealing Directly with Tourists: Marketing Heritage (and Subcomandante Marcos)

### The Santo Domingo Market

Many inexpensive crafts are sold by women sitting in rows that have co-alesced into an enduring crafts market on the grounds around the Santo Domingo church and the old cloister (itself now occupied by the most prestigious co-op, Sna Jolobil). The location is optimal, since tourist traffic is reliably heavy. The market's proximity to Sna Jolobil points up some remarkable contrasts. The huipiles sold in the co-op look like those worn routinely a few generations ago, or in revival today, but the blouses sold outdoors are types that can be made quickly and sold cheaply. But while many items offered in the market are historically inauthentic, the open-air experience is more traditional in the routine hard-edged bargaining and in aspects of the ambience that intrigue some tourists and repulse others: crowds, noise, and dirt. Last, whereas the women who run Sna Jolobil come from various hamlets, the families who work in the market come from one town, Chamula (although most now reside in San Cristóbal's slums).

While a few stands concentrate on specialized items (e.g., just belts), most offer the same set of products and must catch a customer's eye with the particulars of their displays. Sometimes a purchase is the result of serendipity; the tourist has wandered among near-identical stands for just the right length of time to bring emotion and wallet into alignment and is ready to make a selection. Blouses sold here are generally of manufactured thread embroidered on cheap muslin. The type of cloth is traditional not in Chamula but in the lowlands, where men in the village used to do seasonal work. Local women would not make such

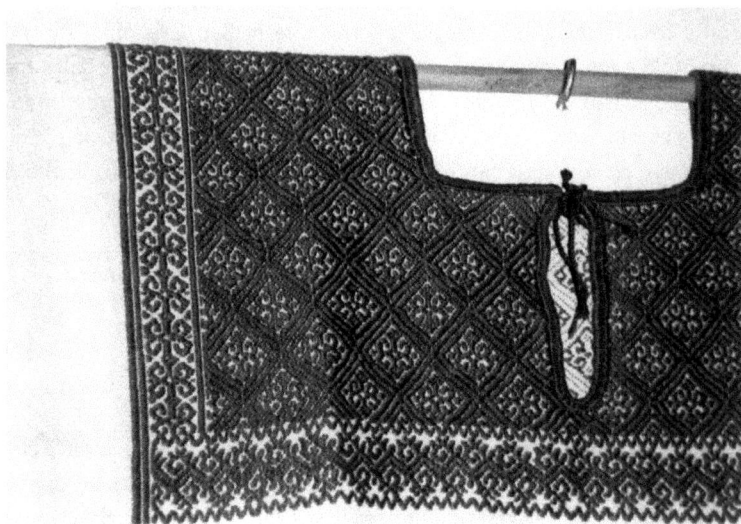

Figure 8. A traditional huipil from the village of Bochil, employing a design reminiscent of, but simpler than, those typical on huipiles from San Andrés Larrainzar.

clothes for their own families—the low prices of the materials would constitute a false economy. But the low quality matters less when foreign bargain hunters buy the blouses as souvenirs rather than to wear them regularly back home. Figures 8–9 show respectively a traditional blouse from Bochil, a village much less accessible than San Andrés, and a much younger—and much more distinctive—design also from there. This second type sells so well in boutiques in San Cristóbal that it is becoming more popular in Bochil itself and is copied by the hundreds by the women exiled from Chamula who dominate the Santo Domingo market.

A second category of goods sold here is sewn toys, little animals and dolls made with scraps of handwoven cloth salvaged from worn-out clothing (figure 10); Indian children play instead with cheap plastic toys.

Half the dolls for sale in 1997 were a new model, the Subcomandante Marcos doll (he is the leader of the antigovernment grassroots Zapatista movement), which achieved instant popularity with politically liberal tourists. This is not to suggest that the Indians either possess or lack

Figure 9. A relatively modern huipil from Bochil, of a type formerly unusual in that village. Brisk sales of huipiles like this one to tourists in San Cristóbal have made the design increasingly popular in Bochil, although tourists seldom venture there.

Figure 10. Stuffed teddy bear made from fragments of worn-out handwoven garments, bought in 1998 from a Chamulan woman in the Santo Domingo open-air market in the center of San Cristóbal. The ears show the pattern most common in many villages, the diamond.

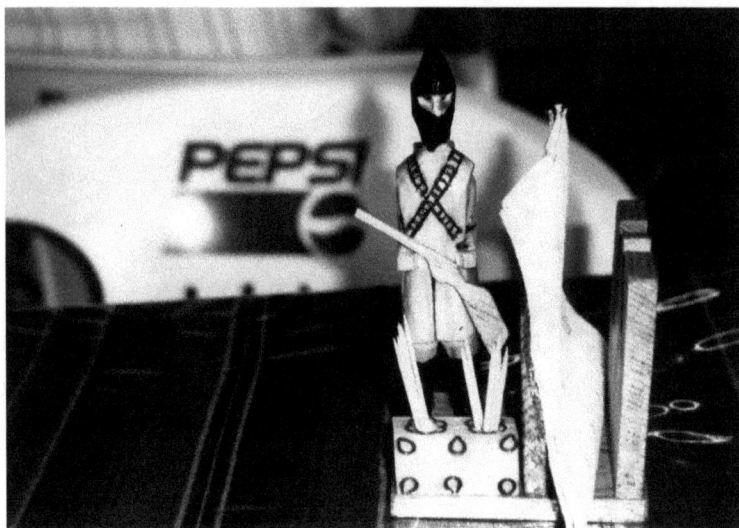

Figure 11. Subcomandante Marcos, leader of the Zapatistas, has become a household totem and highly salable image. Subcomandante Marcos dolls (some on horseback) are sold by dozens of Chamulan women who have sales stations at the Santo Domingo market.

respect for the Subcomandante; rather, the doll illustrates the same willingness to use deeply respected images such as crucifixes and the Virgin Mary as decorations for the dashboards of taxis and buses alongside Disney figurines. The new doll is as abstract as the "ancestors" design— a gun and mask are schematic additions on the same order as the three lines above the man and the corn arms of the woman. The Marcos doll is an apt partner for a similar, commonly sold female doll holding a baby (thus a fertility symbol parallel to that of the corn). Collier mentions that Zapatista images also appeared for a while on condom wrappers (1994, 4). I bought a Marcos baseball hat for a friend and enjoyed dining in a restaurant outfitted with Subcomandante napkin holders (figure 11). Marcos wanted to become a symbolic figure, and he succeeded.

The last classification of goods sold in the Santo Domingo Market comprises miniatures of dolls, hats, pottery, and so on. These and some of the textiles sold by the Chamulan women were made by the only local residents farther down on the socioeconomic scale, Guatemalans living in squalid refugee camps south of San Cristóbal.

*Hawkers*

Young women, often carrying babies, and countless children working alone pursue tourists down the street, energetically marketing woven wristlets and belts for flexible, small fees. Their persistence corners the tourist into an unpleasant choice, either to be rude to the very people he or she has come to see, or to yield to the sales pitch, thereby acknowledging the unpalatable truth that these particular Indians do not embody a comfortable and traditional way of life but rather are painfully poor. Moreover, making a purchase relieves the pressure only temporarily, as it inspires immediate assembly of a crowd of more hawkers (also see Van Den Berghe 1994, 68).

These small weavings are traditional in that they are made on backstrap looms using local wool (though some bracelets have one end just tied to a toe and are woven from there, without a loom). Also, they generally feature the diamond pattern that represents the universe. This might be because this pattern can be shrunk to the smallest size (however, Indian street vendors in Oaxaca weave diamonds less). It is bitterly ironic that while other craftspersons in Chiapas are making a living marketing symbols dear to them, signs of an ethnicity and tradition that they wish to maintain, these mothers and children must sell tiny items representing a way of life that, in many ways, they would dearly love to escape.

### Crafts and Maintaining—or Transforming—a Traditional Way of Life

The average "ethnic" or "cultural" tourist who ventures into the villages surrounding San Cristóbal hopes to witness a mixture of the exotic that they take to be crystallized nostalgia: a simple and fulfilling life on the land. Of course, tourists arriving in Chiapas after the Zapatista uprising began, in 1994, must modify that rosy picture. The fear of stumbling into danger did inhibit tourism briefly, though the rebels took great care not to harm tourists—indeed, supportive international publicity became the best-realized goal of the rebellion. Tourists I encountered in 1997 considered the Zapatistas a romantic eccentricity of the state rather than a threat. However, the disturbance unveiled an ironic truth, that one of the two states in Mexico that best draws visitors seeking an "authentic," peaceful, ethnic idyll is in turmoil. Crafts illustrate this contradiction well: they are especially complex in manufacture and appearance and resonate with religious and local identities precisely because Indians reacted to centuries of political and economic repression by cultivating a vivid and inward-looking ethnicity. How craft objects such as my pillowcase are designed, made, and marketed in modern Chiapas illustrates—indeed, fuels—new trends in power relationships between Indians and outsiders in regard to the transformation of religion, in continuity and change in gender relationships, and in how the individual Indian tries to maintain family and village identity.

*Power*

The defense that ethnicity offered to the Indians of Chiapas against their ill-treatment by the Ladino oligarchy remained a practical and sustainable *psychological* bulwark until recently—it was a strategy that mattered to the Indians, but one that the Ladinos could ignore. Now, since it is how Indians look, their public practice of religion, and their crafts that draw affluent visitors to Chiapas, the Ladino businessmen who run San Cristóbal need the Indians to continue to cultivate their ethnicity. This perpetuates centuries of exploitation: most of the tourist money goes to these Ladinos. But the tourists who observe Indians and buy crafts represent the world outside Chiapas, a world capable of being shocked by how the Indians are treated, and exerting pressure on the Mexican central government for reform. The Zapatistas know this: their strongest weapon is the press communiqué. Last, the Indians limit tourists' access to some of their attractive features and products and thus have slightly more economic leverage with the local power structure than in the past.

Each adult Indian represents a commodity valuable to the government, that is, a vote. Nearly every vote from nearly every Indian community ends up on the PRI section of the ballot. Municipio *caciques*—bilingual Indian intermediaries with considerable power—ensure that the receipt of even the least of government services means a village lined up behind the PRI. But some Indian towns are starting to require more for their votes. For instance, I was told repeatedly that a woman leading a cooperative in one municipio had successfully demanded money for thread and equipment in exchange for continued loyalty.

Most of the paternalistic help that textile cooperatives and cottage industries receive is from Mexicans who came from outside Chiapas and from foreigners. Although any relationship between Indian and outsider is weighted toward the outsider, these strands weaken the historical stranglehold of the local power structure. Through experience with altruistic middlemen, Indians learn business skills that qualify them to work elsewhere. The best intermediaries, like Morris and Past, gradually become dispensable and are happy to turn over well-constructed enterprises to the Indians. This directly affects only a few thousand craftspersons but gives hope to many more. It is important to remember that extensive, minimally exploitative interaction between any outsiders and the Maya is young, and that many of the new supportive relationships concern tourism, especially the production of crafts. Soon there may be more businesses controlled by Indians from bottom to top, from sheep-tending to profit distribution.

*Religion*

Protestant sects continue to make inroads throughout the Maya world, as throughout Latin America. Pentecostals, Presbyterians, Methodists, Baptists, Mormons, Jehovah's Witnesses, and Seventh-Day Adventists all find converts in Chiapas, but it is hard to know how many locals leave Mayan Catholicism because of conviction and how many do so for economic reasons. Two problems plague syncretic Catholicism here. First, plenty of hard liquor (*posh*) must be imbibed during festivals, and many men continue their consumption socially. Alcoholism has been a horrible problem in the highlands (see Eber 1995). It's not as bad today as a few decades ago, owing partly to Protestant preaching against it and partly to a liberal Catholic reaction to losing souls to the Protestants. In particular, an organization called Catholic Action advocates substituting soft drinks for posh in festivals and as routine libations; I saw as much Pepsi as posh in the church in Chamula.

The second vulnerability of Mayan Catholicism is the cargo system. Even as incomes fell, the caciques who control the sales of festival essentials (fireworks, posh, flowers, candles) extorted more money for these goods and organized paramilitary forces to keep the cargo system running smoothly. In several communities, notably Chamula, thousands of Protestants who exited the cargo system were expelled by these bands of thugs. Perhaps twenty-five thousand refugees have ended up in the slums around San Cristóbal. They seek wage labor, but with mixed success. Most of the women and children pressing woven wristlets on tourists are Protestant refugees.

In some villages, and in cooperatives such as Sna Jolobil and cottage industries like Kun Kun, traditional Maya Catholics, members of Catholic Action, and Protestants work side by side. They are all Indians, and they share a past, even if their futures diverge. Many converts are "economic" Protestants. For them, dropping out of the cargo system came first: their falling incomes couldn't keep up with rising expenses. The Protestants offered spiritual refuge and much-needed hospitality in San Cristóbal. Women who are economic Protestants attend their new churches but also pay heed to older religion when they weave patterns like "ancestors."

## Gender

A few generations ago, Indian men earned some outside income, while Indian women stayed home grinding corn, fetching water and firewood, and weaving their families' clothing. The men considered themselves farmers, but Ladino landowners kept Indians from acquiring substantial tracts of arable land. For generations, the average Maya farmer cultivated one small plot of rocky soil in the highlands and another in the lowlands and might have found seasonal work on lowland coffee plantations. Today, lowland plots are fewer, many coffee plantations have become cattle ranches (which need fewer workers), and desperate Guatemalan refugees have taken much of the work on the remaining plantations. Highland men may find other wage labor, particularly in construction, but overall their incomes are shrinking.

Tourists buy textiles made by women, who then feel "capable and productive" by carrying on tradition-sanctioned work in a time-honored way (Eber and Rosenbaum 1993, 165), and they can now help with family expenses. But this traditional women's work has expanded to occupy untraditionally large blocks of time. Sometimes it pays enough that women cannot afford to weave for their husbands and children, instead buying cheap, used town clothes; I saw this especially in Chamula and among refugees from there. Underemployed men dislike these changes. They resent the very thought of fetching water or firewood. Several wives who have taken on a sort of secular cargo by becoming leaders in cooperatives have thereby earned savage beatings. But selling textiles has given women the new option of remaining single. "Why should I marry a drunk?" is an occasionally heard reaction to a widespread problem that many women could not avoid in earlier days (Morris 1987, 70).

Formerly, men linked the family to the outside world, to other villages, to the cities where they might find work, and to the spiritual world: hence the three lines constituting the body of the male figure in "ancestors," and his arms raised heavenward, while the female figure enfolds corn at home. Through commercial weaving, particular in the co-ops formed to serve the tourist market, women who would formerly not have had the self-confidence or opportunity to talk to women from other communities are working and socializing together (Morris 1987, 46). Just a few years ago, a woman who wove "ancestors" into a huipil that she would wear wrapped herself in the traditional role described in that pattern. Now a woman who makes such a huipil for sale or decorates an object such as a pillowcase, something that only an outsider would use, can honor the ancestors while she works but can conceive of living a life different from the life her patterns depict. Weaving for cash takes her beyond the nurturing of corn.

How surprising is the shift in gender roles attendant on the growth of income from women's crafts? The old roles could not be sustained in the economic present. Another model for revised gender roles might be how the sexes relate in the city, but that would constitute a more radical shift than the one caused by working in crafts. Pursuing another visible alternative, exemplified by the Zapatista forces, would be even more wrenching. Women make up perhaps a third of that army and even lead some squads, causing problems even in that "revolutionary" organization. The recasting of gender roles seen in craft villages in the highlands may be the minimum possible in these changing times.

## Village and Family

The many Maya individuals, families, and villages who wish to hold fast to inherited identity as the world changes swiftly around them do as their ancestors did: they armor themselves in their ethnic heritage. They do this in many ways, some of which resemble the processes by which crafts are intensified. First, intensification through virtuosity offers the easiest parallel, when individuals and groups self-consciously and energetically cultivate knowledge of tradition and expertise in crafts. The huipiles sold in Sna Jolobil that illustrate intensification through virtuosity are made by weavers who embody the behavioral form of this process. Second, people can create intensification through addition by wearing more ethnically specific garments than in generations past, by making a point of speaking Tzotzil or Tzeltal when using Spanish would be as easy, and so on. Last, the intensification through selection so important in shaping my pillowcase is enacted by innumerable Maya every day, when, for instance, they spend more time doing ethnicity-specific tasks, like weaving, than did their mothers, but are happy to give up their mothers' other daily routines, such as fetching water.

Christine Eber and Brenda Rosenbaum, who studied cooperatives in Chiapas during the 1970s and 1980s, found that weavers did not "talk about personal empowerment through the symbols they weave [or] the solidarity they create" but rather spoke of "service to the families and communities, at once practical and sacred" (1993, 175). Payment for handmade textiles remains absurdly low but nevertheless buttresses fragile family finances. And though booming populations still require out-migration to prevent famine, income from crafts keeps some families and villages largely intact. In short, engagement with traditional crafts has become critical to these Indians' having any chance of maintaining the first ingredient of a traditional way of life, the traditional community.

The municipios where crafts help stabilize incomes and community, where hope for improved standards of living has thereby been rekindled—in other words, the municipios with something to lose—may be the ones least likely to support radical change. San Andrés Larrainzar, where my pillowcase was made, is such a community. It maintains a long history of flourishing cooperatives, has a firm hold on the aesthetic center of the weaving revival—"ancestors" is just one of the lovely patterns associated with this municipio—and has endured many of the difficult changes in gender relationships and other adjustments connected with shifting from a subsistence to a market economy. Its neighbor, Chenalhó, represents the many municipios that aspire to the success of San Andrés. Indeed, as early as 1989, Eber and Rosenbaum found four weaving cooperatives in Chenalhó (1993, 167). But traditional weavings from this municipio are not as appealing as those from San Andrés, both to my eye and in the cumulative opinion of tourists as expressed in how much space is allotted Chenalhó's weavings in Sna Jolobil (much less than for San Andrés) and in the Casa de Artesanias (none). Weavers from Chenalhó have not been able to garner nearly as much craft-based income as have the truly successful craft villages (167, 173).

The massacre in an outlying hamlet of Chenalhó may be interpreted as having resulted from the clash of views concerning how Indians can improve their collective lot. The crafts movement offers modest incomes and the prospect of gradual betterment. While the money earned is seldom substantial, it has the advantage of originating for the most part outside the country, independent of the vicissitudes of the Mexican economy. Conversely, the Zapatistas insist on dramatic and immediate change. The national government responded to the rebellion with its own rhetoric and with an effective strategy of double containment. Mexican troops now surround the Zapatista army, and the villages just outside the revolutionary forces' rural enclaves are receiving money for jobs, housing, social services, and infrastructure such as roads, government-run stores, and potable water systems (Russell 1995, 84). The villagers welcome this money but consider it overdue and apt to evaporate when the immediate crisis subsides.

The Zapatistas rub conservative Indians the wrong way by, for instance, elevating women into positions of command: having women assume responsibility in weaving collectives has been grating enough. Worst of all, the very flare-ups in publicity that inspire some cynical government expenditures drive away large numbers of tourists, thereby abruptly depressing the economy of the entire highlands. The men who attacked the municipio's outlying hamlet of Acteal at the end of

1997 were not just following the orders of rapacious caciques; they were fighting against a community whose sheltering of Indians sympathetic to the Zapatistas could be seen as taking food out of their own families' mouths. In such incidents, Indians who want food, land, and the chance to retain some measure of traditional identity are pitted against other Indians who have the same desires, but different ideas about how to attain those goals.

Pierre Van Den Berghe ends his book on tourism in San Cristóbal (1994) with a section titled "What Went Right?" He cites factors that include an optimal degree of outsider access to the area, the intrinsic attractiveness of the Indians, climate, and scenery that "ethnic" tourists are not apt to pollute, and the sensibly small scale of ongoing local development (147–51). My argument, in contrast, has focused on how the "attractiveness" of the Indians to tourists stems from long-term oppression, and on how, despite the great degree to which the tourist industry perpetuates historical exploitation, making crafts can be done in a way that "selling tradition" does not injure it significantly. Moreover, the modest income from crafts helps protect aspects of traditional life. The Zapatistas desire faster and more comprehensive improvements. Which combination of paths to sorely needed change will prove most valuable is impossible to predict. Some form of armed struggle will continue— after all, this too is part of local tradition. At the same time, tourism and sales of crafts will continue to offer modest, steady support for gradual change in the highlands. In the coming chapters, I will examine how these factors play out in Oaxaca, a field that is larger and more complex in various ways.

# 2.

# Crafts and Tourism in Oaxaca

Indian hunter-gatherers lived in Oaxaca as early as twenty thousand years ago and added agriculture to their strategies for survival as early as 7000 BC. The "three sisters" that sustain many peasants today—corn, beans, and squash—have been staples for at least as long as villages have existed, that is, since about 2000 BC. To hunt they had spears and bows and arrows; to cultivate they had digging sticks. Many other tools must have been part of daily life long before traces of them were left for archaeologists to find. At some point the Indians began making their everyday objects with techniques and results that reached beyond the purely utilitarian; they added creative panache to the building process and thus were making crafts artfully.

### Crafts in the History of Oaxaca through the Advent of Tourism

The oldest surviving exemplars of the main southern Mexican craft categories are shards of pottery; a few ceramic figures that also bear depictions of cloth skirts, sandals, and jewelry. The need for furniture required carving wood. Burials with jewelry, favorite possessions, and food and drink constitute our first evidence of ritual. By about 500 BC, villages grew from handfuls of dwellings to clusters of several hundred residents, and social classes began to emerge. For example, a village near the current site of the city of Oaxaca housed specialists who cut and polished magnetite into mirrors for trade (Whipperman 2000, 18). And some of the early pottery illustrates differentiation between rather plain, functional pieces and finer, more decorated ones for the upper classes.

The fertile Oaxaca valleys nourished an increasingly stratified society, one headed by priests and soldiers but also including architects and artists. A calendar rationalized the yearly cycle of events, and written script eventually came into being. Ancestors of Oaxaca's Zapotec Indians founded Monte Albán above the junction of the three central valleys. This and a dozen smaller ritual and administrative centers flourished on defensible hilltops through about AD 750. During the peak of population, roughly AD 500 through 750, social differentiation was also relatively great. As one consequence, pottery became relatively elaborate (Murphy and Stepick 1991, 14). War was a constant, but why this civilization dissolved remains unclear, as mysterious as the demise of the Mayan empire in Chiapas and the Yucatán, and of Teotihuacán in the central valley of Mexico. Throughout Mexico, cities that had been vassals became independent states. In this Zapotec territory, the lack of focused power invited invasion by the nascent Mixtec people, gathered together by the warlord known in surviving codices as Tiger Claw. Mixtec nobles forced marriage with Zapotec heiresses. Although few Mixtec speakers remain in the central valleys today, both ruins and modern crafts display a fascinating mix of Zapotec and Mixtec artistic traditions.

The Aztecs arrived in the valley of Mexico around 1250 and ruled it within a century. As part of a general expansion of their territory, they subjugated the city of Oaxaca during the 1400s, establishing a garrison at the site of present-day Oaxaca by midcentury. Tribute paid by the Zapotecs took various forms depending on what a village had to offer. Teotitlán del Valle, located about thirty kilometers outside Oaxaca, sent four hundred bundles of embroidered cotton fabric and eight hundred bundles of wider fabric every three months, according to an exhibit in modern Teotitlán's municipal museum.

The Aztecs' energetic combination of war, diplomacy, and forced political marriages was never enough to subjugate the entire state of Oaxaca. The conquistadores would be more successful. The chronology is compelling: Cortés and his band of adventurers arrived from Cuba near present-day Veracruz in 1519 and took over the Aztec capital of Tenochtitlán by 1521. A central strategy was to gather allies from peoples subject to the Aztecs, including the Zapotecs (though the Mixtecs initially resisted). By the end of 1521, the Catholic mass had been celebrated in the region of Oaxaca, and the Spanish were firmly in power throughout the state within months. When Cortés presented New Spain to his king, he claimed a reward: the valley of Oaxaca. He received rights to most of the good valley land and would himself grant *encomiendas* (rights to land and the labor of the resident Indians) to friends, relatives, and children. However, Spanish squatters repeatedly occupied the site of the old Aztec garrison and were eventually allowed to remain there. Their town, Antequera, became the city of Oaxaca.

The Spanish commanded garrisons, large ranches, and anything resembling a cash economy, and they controlled many Indians on their haciendas. But they had little to do with the rest of the native population, which, while dramatically diminished by disease, still vastly outnumbered the colonizers. Much of the work of integration, reorganization, and assimilation devolved on missionaries—in Oaxaca, especially the Dominicans. They wanted to save both souls and bodies and took flexible and practical approaches to these linked tasks. They were able to teach dogma and ritual because they learned and employed Indian languages, even as the Indians acquired Spanish. As in many parts of the world colonized by Catholics, native religion soon mixed Christian and pagan elements; adopted European saints and ceremonies bore both overt and less-obvious native personalities and characteristics. The missionaries also both learned from and transformed local agriculture and crafts. Oaxacan tomatoes and peppers went to Europe, but the top export was the red dye called cochineal. The church fathers encouraged many villages to concentrate on one or another craft for purposes of commerce, often building on preexistent specializations. For instance, while working with wool was new in the Oaxaca village of Teotitlán del Valle—sheep arrived with the Spaniards—weaving cotton was already important there. And the residents of the pottery center Santa María Atzompa, which rests on the unexcavated outskirts of Monte Albán, were encouraged to continue to specialize in that craft.

The dynamics among transplanted Spaniards evolved swiftly. Newly arriving authorities guarding the king of Spain's interests curbed the powers of the rapacious conquistadores, and secular and sacred authorities also clashed. Conflicts between various groups often focused on the treatment of Indians. Agents of the crown took a longer view than did the conquerors—working Indians to death was bad economics—and the clergy, following the lead of the Dominican Bartolomé de Las Casas, favored humane treatment of the "savages."

Oaxaca's importance waxed and waned. The city lost its function as a pivotal southern trade station to Acapulco in the late sixteenth century. A promising silk industry in the mountainous Mixtec region of the state lasted only from about 1548 to about 1570; abused Indian workers soon rebelled and cut down the mulberry trees sustaining the silkworms. But silk weaving did not die out completely, and this abortive attempt to found one kind of weaving industry set a foundation for a broader effort using wool and cotton, one linked strongly to the ready availability of cochineal. There were over five hundred cotton or silk looms in the city of Oaxaca by 1792, and Indians were forced to produce cochineal in an oppressive system similar in terms of economics to sharecropping in the southern United States (Murphy and Stepick 1991, 27). Then the Wars of Independence squelched cochineal and other Mexican industries after 1810, and most cochineal production shifted to Guatemala. During a brief period of stability while the Oaxaca native Benito Juárez was president of Mexico (1848–52), crafts centers including Atzompa temporarily reattained some level of economic viability. But for most of the nineteenth century, Oaxaca shared in the turmoil that kept Mexico from emerging from poverty. The arrival of a railroad line in 1892 gave the local elite access to foreign goods, but there was less economic progress and change overall than in northern and central parts of Mexico (Murphy and Stepick 1991, 32).

Little violence disturbed Oaxaca during the Mexican revolution in the second and third decades of the twentieth century. That lack of disturbance was positive at the time but had an unfortunate aftereffect. The leaders of the country during those times acquired no special affection for the state for this reason (peace meant nonparticipation in the revolution) and other reasons as well (Oaxacans made a few ineffectual attempts to break the state away from Mexico), leaving Oaxaca underfunded by the federal government. Persistent social and economic inequality yielded sporadic unrest, which resulted in the army frequently occupying the city center during the remainder of the century: in 1950, to resolve a dispute between coffee growers and Oaxaca's elite, during a land-squatting episode in the 1970s, and so on. Oaxaca has been slow to recover from such times and from periodic economic crises, in part due to the lack of significant industrial activity.

When the Pan-American Highway arrived in Oaxaca in 1948, manu-factured goods like plaid dresses, cheap shoes, and plastic or inexpen-sive porcelain kitchenware became more readily available to the general populace, though the industries producing such goods did not arrive along with the products. At that time, there was little reason to invest in this city, which, while located in a pleasant complex of valleys, was surrounded by mountains traversed only by endless curves of narrow roads. There was a potential advantage in this: being able to pay wages lower than the average for Mexico; per capita income in Oaxaca has long hovered at about a third of the national average (Hulshof 1991, 21). But the advantage of lower pay was more than erased by the geographic disadvantage: transportation expenses would have eaten into profits too much. Indeed, there is still no significant industry in Oaxaca, and sub-sistence agriculture is simply not enough to support the populace (14). Tourism fuels the economy now, though this factor mainly affects the central valleys, a few beach resorts, and cities along the highways.

### Crafts in Modern Oaxaca: The Example of Black Pottery

How do crafts fit into the broader socioeconomic landscape today? With most portable necessities owned by the working class now avail-able as cheap manufactured imports, continuing to make many things by hand for *local* use became an unaffordable luxury. But mass-pro-duced goods arrived so recently that the physical and mental habits of personal craftsmanship never passed from living memory. And certain crafts were never displaced completely. These included items important for maintaining a sense of regional identity, such as handwoven clothes worn for ceremonial purposes (though daily wear shifted to cheap im-ports), and articles occupying specialized niches, such as pots made in shapes and sizes not readily available in plastic or aluminum. Indeed, the minimal extent of industrial development in Oaxaca meant that the occupation of handmaking crafts could not be as swiftly or fully abandoned in favor of factory jobs as had become common elsewhere. At the same time, mass-produced imports could not always substitute for locally handmade products. For instance, weavers of serapes further north, in Tlaxcolo and Texcoco, gave up that craft in the 1950s in favor of the improved wages available due to the burgeoning of industry there. In contrast, weavers in Oaxaca's Teotitlán had far fewer such lucrative alternatives for employment, and, in a complementary factor, there was still some call for serapes for local use. Yes, cheap coats were available, but the convenient shape of the serape and the fact that serapes shed water effectively made them better for much outdoor work, and Oaxacans would make them for lower wages than were now acceptable in the north and central parts of the country.

Tourism became a major global industry following World War II (Cohen 2004, 1). The same trains and trucks that conveyed manufactured goods to Oaxaca also began to deliver a trickle of tourists from more prosperous parts of Mexico. That trickle became a rivulet when air travel became feasible around 1970, and steadily increased thereafter. In contrast to Chiapas, a majority of the tourists visiting Oaxaca remain Mexican nationals, though U.S. citizens and somewhat fewer Europeans are important constituencies and are critical in the support of craft communities. Tourists who fly in can buy souvenirs in the airport in booths freely juxtaposing both local and national crafts with generic souvenirs (T-shirts, etc.) in a compact preview of shopping opportunities to come. They also immediately see references to the Guelaguetza, the splendid local festival encompassing Mexico's most extensive and colorful variety of dance performances. Indeed, many tourists planning trips to Oaxaca come in July so that they can attend one of these massive shows.

The factors that discouraged economic growth for so long dovetail with those that encourage and nourish ethnic tourism. The black pottery of San Bartolo Coyotepec offers the simplest illustration of this. Coyotepec had long been a center for the production of large, sturdy gray pottery containers for mescal or other liquids, these pots being ideal for portage by mules. But these containers' function was assumed by lighter, inexpensive plastic jugs in the late 1940s. Could the potters of Coyotepec survive as such? One woman found an answer. In the early 1950s, Doña Rosa Valente e Nieto changed her technique in two ways.

First, she polished the exterior of a pot with a smooth chunk of quartz before firing, which imparted an added luster. Her second innovation built on a peculiarity of local firing; that is, the Coyotepec potters used wood-burning, low-oxygen kilns, which contributed enough carbon to the pots' surfaces to turn what would otherwise have been reddish-tan products dark gray. Doña Rosa fired a few pots for six to eight hours rather than the customary twelve to fourteen and got beautiful black pots rather than gray ones. This was a more radical change than had resulted from her polishing pots before firing, because the gorgeous underfired black pots did not hold water. Adopting this technique thus explicitly traded historical function for the enhanced appearance that made these pots desirable souvenirs. We will see that such dramatic ruptures are not exceptional but instead quite typical of the changes made as crafts move from practical uses in insiders' daily lives to satisfying the aesthetic needs of outsiders. Those customers also have ideological needs, perhaps vaguely felt and expressed, but still critical: they need to believe that crafts they buy illustrate considerable continuity in the lives of their makers. Coping with this issue entails artful compromises and allowances. Here, signs in the large store run by Doña Rosa's family simply state that the pots are not watertight—the customer is left to speculate why and to choose whether or not to mull over the fact that the pretty black base color of the pots is produced by an "inauthentic" technique.

Has black pottery experienced folkloric intensification in a manner similar to the pillowcase I discussed in the previous chapter? As a genre it has, though different pots exhibit different types of intensification and combinations of types. I will postpone classifying these until near the end of this chapter, but I will note here that most pieces of black pottery made today are much smaller than the ancestral gray pots—some are true miniatures—and that nearly every piece is more elaborate than those pretourism models. For instance, the black pot shown in figure 13 is a curved object whose shape is reinforced—indeed, intensified— by the decorative cutouts, themselves curved. Other common shapes include candleholders, pitchers, and vases that look as if they should be able to hold water and flowers but actually require plastic inserts to do so. In addition, there are ashtrays, food-serving trays, lamp bases, and

Figure 12. Valente Nieto Real, incising and superimposing decorations on a newly shaped pot during a demonstration for tourists at the family factory and showroom in San Bartolo Coyotepec (just a short bus ride south of the city of Oaxaca). In lieu of a mechanical potter's wheel, potters in this village manually spin a plate balanced on another, inverted plate.

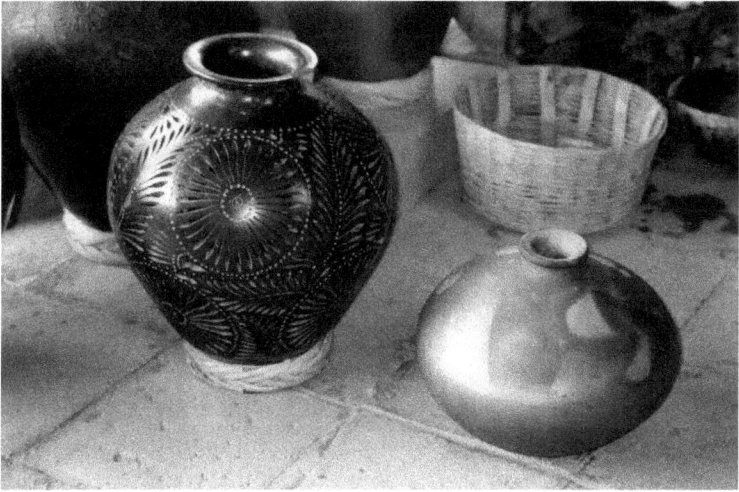

Figure 13. New and older-style pots shown as part of Valente's demonstration. The more traditional gray pot is fired about sixteen hours and is watertight. Valente's mother, Doña Rosa Valente e Nieto, invented the technique of making shinier, blacker pottery. The cutout decorations on the pot seen here do not actually detract from function, since the shorter firing time for the black pots has already rendered them not watertight.

all sorts of sculptures done largely in black. Supplementing the proliferation of shapes, the basic black can be varied by adding tints to sections (often to achieve a mosaic effect) and even gold leaf.

Coyotepec can stand for many a craft village in the central valleys in both layout of the town and typical sales techniques. It has a fine location for a short day trip from Oaxaca and also ensnares car travelers headed south from town. It straddles the Pan-American Highway about twelve kilometers south of the city of Oaxaca and thus is on the way to Teotitlán del Valle, to the ruins and modern city of Mitla, and, if one were to travel another twelve to fourteen hours, to San Cristóbal de las Casas. The main craft market is visible from the highway. A dozen stalls contain a good variety of pottery for the buyer in a hurry, though most shoppers will proceed down the main street perpendicular to the highway and visit the large establishment owned by the family of Doña Rosa. There is a large parking lot and a single entrance to the extensive central courtyard, one big enough for grass, trees, and a pile of the old large gray pots. In the shaded corridors surrounding the green area and in several rooms off those corridors, one finds endless rows of black pottery for sale, grouped by size and type. Newspaper articles about Doña Rosa are displayed in a prominent spot, as is a diploma praising her pioneering work.

Making many dozens of new pots every day—this is a volume business—is done by a half-dozen family members out of public view. However, Doña Rosa's eldest son, Valente Nieto, gives a lecture-demonstration two or three times a day. My pictures of a moment from that show (figures 12–13) are similar to thousands of photos taken by other visitors. Nieto takes out a pair of large, shallow saucers that constitute a foot-twirled substitute for a potter's wheel, shapes a chunk of clay on this odd, improvised-looking device, and goes through all the steps to make a good-sized pitcher. Of course, when such pots are actually made, pauses of prescribed numbers of days separate these steps. Nieto's demonstration skips those required drying intervals by having partly finished pots at the ready to continue the lecture, much as in televised cooking shows that condense long processes into a few minutes each. His end result is a compact but authentic-seeming learning experience for a few dozen visitors, who can then feel a greater connection to the pots they invariably buy.

Each of the many crafts and craft communities in the state of Oaxaca reflects much of these same processes and, when the villages are similarly easy for tourists to visit, parallel sales strategies. Black pottery is the simplest to discuss of the main crafts whose primary home is the central valleys of Oaxaca, but the central themes of its history, production, and sales strategies are common to each of the other crafts of the valleys.

## Rugs: Invention, Designs, Dyes

The most prestigious, most widely known, and overall most expensive crafts made in the state of Oaxaca are the handwoven rugs of Teotitlán del Valle (about thirty kilometers south of Oaxaca, just off the Pan-American Highway) and of its less famous, slightly less accessible neighbor, Santa Ana del Valle; rugs are also made piecemeal in a few other villages. Rugs are not common in working-class Mexican homes,

particularly in rural areas. Floors made of tile or other waterproof surfaces (presuming a family is affluent enough to not settle for a dirt floor)
are mopped every day and do not constitute a natural environment for
fine textiles. Nevertheless these rugs are broadly taken to be a venerable
local folk art.

Publications about the weavings of Teotitlán del Valle and the captions
accompanying exhibits in the rug museums there and in Santa Ana del
Valle all offer roughly the same narrative: Teotitlán has an ancient weaving tradition (Santa Ana markets most of its products through middlemen in Teotitlán and in the larger nearby market town of Tlacolula and
is not mentioned in Teotitlán's museum). The Spanish brought in the
pedal loom and sheep, serapes became the central product of the village, and rugs are made there today in a wonderful variety of designs—
many having one or another historical basis or inspiration—and featuring natural dyes. The leap in the customary narrative from serape to
rug seems not to injure the twin themes of continuity and authenticity,
although the weaving of rugs constitutes a dramatic break in tradition.[1]
How did it happen? According to local oral tradition, Ismael Gutiérrez,
a taxi driver who was transplanted to the United States after World War
II, noted the use of area rugs in North American homes and returned to
Teotitlán in the 1960s with that knowledge as an inspiration for revital-
izing the local weaving business (Scott Roth, quoted in Stanton 1999,
43). If this story is accurate—as least as far as the timing goes—then the
rug-weaving tradition as a practice separate from the earlier making of
serapes is just under a half-century old, a few years junior to Coyotepec's black pottery. Other parts of the standard story are vulnerable,
too. Many of the supposedly historical designs used today were actually
introduced by importers and are based on the William Randolph Hearst
textile collection, just as many or most weavers still use synthetic dyes
(Stanton, personal communication, September 25, 2008). Nevertheless
the basic narrative endures, quietly skirting these inconvenient facts.

An informal but energetic committee of Oaxacan intellectuals and
Teotitlán leaders—Stanton mentions the famous painters Francisco To-
ledo and Rufino Tamayo and the Zapotec weaver Isaac Vásquez (Stanton 1999, 101)—did revive the natural dyes that had gone out of general
use with the arrival of aniline dyes in the mid-nineteenth century, and

added many designs to the few inherited from the local serape-weaving tradition. Tourists from central and northern Mexico bought some rugs during the late 1960s and 1970s, and the market expanded considerably when tourism from the United States blossomed in the 1980s (this happening partly due to serious economic problems in Mexico that increased the buying power of the dollar). A rug market (about a dozen booths) was added to the town center in 1985, and a small rug museum opened ten years later.

Today tourists can drive to Teotitlán or take one of a half-dozen buses that travel daily to the village from Oaxaca's busy second-class bus station. Alternatively, they may hop one of dozens of other intercity buses to the corner of the Pan-American Highway and the four-kilometer road to the village, then take a shuttle taxi up the hill into town. Signs advertising rug shops are visible from the highway, and stores fronting on the artery that links highway and town are decorated to attract tourists. Families who own home-studios on the main drags (the road into town, the street perpendicular to that one going the few blocks to the center, and the cross street from there uphill to the church and market), advertise their wares on signs, hang rugs where they can be seen from the street, and leave doors invitingly open.

If no family member happens to be weaving when a tourist wanders in, one will probably quickly get into action. Demonstrating the intricate weaving process on the massive looms engages the prospective customer in the creative process and also illustrates that these weavings take plenty of labor to make (justifying prices). Dyed yarn may also be displayed, and perhaps even a chunk or two of the prickly-pear cactus that is home to the minute insect from which cochineal red dye is made, all in the service of capturing the tourist's attention and thus patronage. Sales pitches generally begin with an assertion that natural dyes including cochineal were used during the dyeing process (whether true or not). The ensuing sales choreography matches that of many places in the world where rugs are handmade: the salesperson quickly yet artfully lays out lots of rugs, asking which ones the observer prefers, thus trying to shift the decision-making process from *if* there will be a sale to *which* item will be bought.

I chose the rugs to be represented in photographs in this book partly due to affection, but even more so because they illustrate important factors in how these weavings are designed, created, and marketed. The reader should locate and glance at the following photographs before continuing.

Figure 1. Felipe Hernández's sons, two small rugs.

Figure 14. Mendoza family, a variety of rugs.

Figure 16. José Gonzales, showing Ellen Goertzen how to weave. Behind them is a Navajo-themed rug, showing Yeis (supernatural beings said to have the power to heal).

Figure 17. José de los Angeles, rug showing birds and flowers in undyed tints of wool.

Figure 18. Felipe Hernández, rug in original design, in his store in downtown Oaxaca.

Figure 19. Isabel Gutierrez, many rugs, especially ones imitating famous paintings, on display in the extended family's stall in the rug market in central Teotitlán.

Figure 23. Arnulfo Mendoza, silk-and-wool rug shown as backdrop in photo of his wife Mary Jane Gagnier-Mendoza, in Mano Mágica, their high-end craft store in downtown Oaxaca.

Figure 32. Isabel Gutierrez, wide variety of sizes and types of rugs, on display in the family's sales stall in 2007 (a leaner year than when the photograph in figure 19 was taken).

When my family and I visited the Mendoza family home-studio in May 1999, the clan leader Arnulfo Mendoza (not closely related to the famous Arnulfo Mendoza of figure 23) quickly laid out plenty of rugs in the middle of the courtyard, following the standard sales strategy (figure 14). This array offered no surprises in terms of sizes, shapes, colors, or designs. A typical rug made in Teotitlán is about 30 inches by 56–57 inches, as are several of these. The one in the foreground is a longer one for a hallway, and a couple of rugs are a bit wider than the norm, to suit the nearly square central decorative figuration.

Well over half of the rugs made in Teotitlán contain geometric designs similar to the ones in this array. Several elements reproduce design elements covering the ruins at Mitla, twenty kilometers away, and found

Figure 14. Wool rugs bearing a representative variety of geometric patterns displayed for the Goertzen family's delectation in the patio of the Arnulfo Mendoza family (not the famous Arnulfo) in Teotitlán del Valle, December 1999. The common sales technique of quickly laying out lots of rugs attempts to change one question in the customer's mind—*if* they are serious about buying something—to another question: *which* rug they like the most and thus might be convinced to purchase.

Figure 15. Mitla, a ruin about thirty kilometers from Teotitlán, is covered with these patterns. Many of the same patterns have also been found on stones beneath or near the church in Teotitlán. Churches were routinely built on the sites of dismantled pyramids—and are cited in weavers' narratives about their products. Some of these decorated stones are now set into the outside of the exterior wall of that church.

on stones implanted in the stucco exterior of the church in Teotitlán. These stones bear most of the Mitla designs and are stones left over from the ruins on top of which the church was built.

Compare the *grecas* (stepped frets) from Mitla (figure 15) with those in the rug that is the second to the farthest back; grecas may be the most common design motif in rugs from Teotitlán. That rug also features several examples of the nested-cross motif common in Mitla (and present in several fragments from the Teotitlán ruins). Serrated diamonds such as those in the weavings closest to the camera are used in rugs in many cultures; this design element may have come to Teotitlán as part of a broad Navajo influence that began early in the rug revival of the late 1960s and early 1970s, an influence that shows no sign of abating. The rug farthest from the camera stands for many that illustrate the Navajo link; it combines elements typical of the two most famous regional Navajo rug substyles, the Two Grey Hills and Ganado Red types, which share many design elements but are distinguished by dye choices (such regional Navajo substyles are easily sampled through U.S. stores' Web sites). This rug has some undyed wool colors, reflecting the Two Grey Hills substyle; some reds, perhaps bowing to the Ganado Red type; and some other colors, too. Last, the remaining rug that we see most of in the photo, the one positioned between the "diamonds" pair and the rug with a flower and crosses, is an original design based on the ubiquitous diamond motif.

Many of the designs on other rugs pictured in my photographs can be understood with reference to those spread out on the Mendoza's patio. But two broad classifications are not represented there. First, quite a few rugs feature Mexican themes copied from ancient clay tablets or from codices: stylized eagles, snakes, jaguars, and so on. These themes, Mexican but not from around Teotitlán, reflect national patriotism filtered through intellectuals' involvement in the rug revival in the 1960s and 1970s. Last, we see representatives of a perhaps surprising and yet very common strategy, the weaving of copies of or designs derived from twentieth-century paintings or murals, particularly ones by M. C. Escher, Diego Rivera, and less frequently Picasso or Miró. Escher-derived interlocking fish such as those in the rug held by Isabel Gutierrez are the most common design in this classification (ones in which a school of fish interlocks with a flock of birds, as in the second photo of Gutierrez [figure 32] are rarer). Closely following the Escher fish in popularity are versions of Rivera's woman with lilies (a theme common in his work).

Where is Zapotec heritage and creativity in all of this? For many centuries, the Zapotecs have been under some other population's rule and have managed to balance pleasing those in power with pride in self-expression. That is precisely what we see taking place in the rugs. Just a few of the designs reflect pre-Columbian local history. But those frets (grecas) and crosses appear everywhere, both singly and conjoined with designs from elsewhere. Syntheses of designs and, above all, the colors chosen mark rugs as being from here. That is especially easy to see in the Navajo designs, which have been important for contributing themes and stimulating creativity throughout the history of Zapotec rugs. It is true that some of Teotitlán weavers' Navajo work is meant simply to counterfeit Navajo rugs, although knowledgeable buyers in the United

Figure 16. Much of the appeal of visiting villages to buy crafts is to witness craftsmen at work. In Teotitlán del Valle, several looms will likely be in use at any given daylight hour in each family's patio-salesroom. Here José Gonzales shows Ellen Goertzen how to weave in 1999. He doesn't waste any yarn: the rug on the loom bears an intimate mix of colors created by linking strands of yarn left over from other rugs, an "end-of-day" approach common in many crafts. The rug hanging on the wall has a Navajo subject but a Zapotec border.

Figure 17. Rug made by José de los Angeles and family of Teotitlán, woven entirely from undyed wool. Different customers have different preferences in terms of colors and patterns, as well as contrasting, ardently held views of what makes a craft truly "authentic." Most weaving families try to serve all possible customers, regardless of their varying aesthetic and ideological orientations.

Figure 18. Felipe Hernández, in front of a rug made to his own original pattern, for sale in his store in Oaxaca city in the summer of 2000. The large figure dominating the rug is a stylized tarantula, and the smaller figures at the center of the top and bottom are grasshoppers, both his own designs. Hernández prefers to make his own artistic decisions, as here. However, much of his business is commissioned, with the desired product specified in both pattern (he can work well from computerized directions) and colors (he can match these as well as anyone can).

Figure 19. Isabel Gutierrez, who has sold her family's rugs at a stall in the central Teotitlán rug market (a dozen stalls across from the city museum) since 1980. Among the most expensive rugs for sale in this photo from 1999 are those reproducing famous paintings. Escher's interlocking fish are a common choice, liked by many modern-oriented customers, yet congruent with the ancient local pattern of interlocking grecas, or stepped frets (figures 1 and 14–16). Other painters whose work weavers regularly copy include Miró, Picasso, and Diego Rivera, as in this rug depicting an Indian women kneeling before lilies (an image often borrowed from Rivera).

States can tell Navajo and Zapotec work apart readily, with the most apparent distinction being the different way edges are woven (the Navajo use a different weaving technique on their upright looms; other differences are readily apparent to experts). For many customers, the bottom line is that the dramatic and daunting disparity in cost trumps authenticity. Moderately faithful Zapotec replicas of Navajo rugs are relatively inexpensive, so plenty of those copies are commissioned constantly, many for eventual sale in the U.S. Southwest.

Nearly every weaver in Teotitlán spends plenty of time replicating or freely drawing on Navajo themes, but no one I know emphasizes *only* that side of local weaving. Some weavers work out their compromises within individual rugs. For instance, José Gonzales's photographed Navajo Yei rug has a Zapotec grecas border (figure 16). He's clearly not trying to fool anyone into believing that his work is actually done by a Navajo, and the combination of designs works well. I asked José de los Angeles how much a Navajo design needed to be modified to become acceptably Zapotec. He pointed out that Teotitlán's weavers had been doing work based on Navajo antecedents for a long time and felt comfortable with this. He supported his argument by comparing two rugs made in the family studio. One mirrored a common Navajo model, a series of large, maroon interlocking diamonds with black serrated edges on a white field (one like this is partly visible behind Isabel Gutierrez's head in figure 32). He juxtaposed that copy with another containing the same shapes but including a wider variety of hues, mostly pastels. Color was enough to mark that rug as Zapotec, he felt (for a parallel example, see the Two Grey Hills rug transformed by featuring bright Zapotec dyes in Stanton 1999, 73). Other weavers, like Felipe Hernández, receive commission after commission to copy specific historic Navajo designs precisely (e.g., see Stanton 1999, 64 and 70). His reaction to this intellectually disquieting (but lucrative) creative straitjacket is to make his own designs all the more unusual. The one pictured in figure 18 might exhibit some unconscious Navajo influence, but this composition, featuring stylized tarantulas and grasshoppers, is very much his own and is just one of dozens of remarkably distinctive works.

Now and again I meet a rug collector who turns up his or her nose at Teotitlán rugs due to the frequent echoing of Navajo design elements, the implication being that the Navajo tradition is superior due to an uninterrupted and unsullied Navajo heritage. In this connection, I can do no better than to quote the folklorist Laura Marcus:

During the latter years of the 19th century, increased European settlement and the advent of the railroad and tourism to the Southwest forged a market for Native American arts. A downturn in the wool trade inspired traders to promote weavings as a better return on the Navajo wool harvest. Tapping popular taste for oriental carpets, traders encouraged weavers to make thicker pieces that could serve as floor rugs [and also incorporating oriental design elements]. As the link between weavers and the outside market, traders embraced diverse notions of taste. Regional rug designs named for particular trading posts emerged at this juncture and are still current today. (Marcus n.d., 43)

Previously, Navajo weaving had been strongly influenced by designs from Saltillo, Mexico (Marcus n.d., 35; see also Jeter and Juelke 1978). Then, in the 1920s and 1930s, a series of affluent women patrons from the eastern United States imposed another layer of outside influence. The passage of time has allowed Navajo weaving to shed those eclectic associations, but the true history of Navajo crafts is actually no more innocent of outside influences than is the history of Zapotec crafts.

Even the most modest small rugs woven in Teotitlán are artistically rich. The chair seat–sized rugs shown in figure 1 were woven by Felipe Hernández's young sons, though he chose the designs and colors. The rug on the left in the photograph is nicely poised between function and decoration—it could go on the floor or be displayed on the wall with equal success. The grecas motif from Mitla implies both motion and stasis: the observer's eye both climbs the stairs and receives the embrace of the interlocking design. The gray color of the field and some of the steps (undyed natural wool, as are all the colors in José de los Angeles's rug shown in figure 17) recalls the stone ruins that are the source of the grecas design. The pink, green, and red alternatives move incrementally away from that gray without surprising the eye. Hernández's use of natural dyes is obvious. Of the main colors, his pink is produced by a thin concentration of cochineal on white wool, the red by a more intense cochineal on light gray wool, and the pale green by a mixture of alfalfa and indigo on white wool.

The dyes in the rug on the right of figure 1 are stronger, though involving the same dyestuffs in different strengths and combinations. The more intense colors support a more dramatic design, now with a layered cross as a central focus. This offers both an aesthetic and a religious effect: although crosses are found in the walls of Mitla (and formerly at Teotitlán itself), Zapotecs now associate that symbol mainly with Christianity, so that a rug design like this positions one era of Zapotec history and spirituality flanking another. In both these little rugs, the sizes and locations of main design elements, stripes, and borders all balance well. Part of the difference in these rugs results from Felipe's perception that tourists preferred pastels in 1994 and brighter colors in 1998 (the dates when the two rugs were made).

The dyes symbolize connections with nature and local history. They are more trouble to use than chemical ones, but less taxing on the health of those making the dyes, and do help sales, especially with authenticity-oriented Americans (Europeans and Mexicans care about this factor less or not at all, I was told repeatedly). And some of the design elements bear evocative meanings. Isabel Gutierrez told me in 1998 that the grecas are "como llave" (like keys) "or days of the week, or secret tunnels of life and death." The diamonds represent life and are also literally diamonds, with consequent brilliance, precious tones, and high expense. Arrows (*flechas*) did mean arrows, snails signified nature "and other things," the ancient Mexican motifs evoked history, and as for the European paintings—Isabel just shrugged.

It is quite a distance in terms of size, level of detail, and cost from these small rugs to the masterpiece by Arnulfo Mendoza pictured in figure 23. His intricate silk weavings, many of which resemble this one in that they draw on historic serape patterns from Saltillo (and elsewhere in Mexico, but the ones from Saltillo survived in greater numbers; see Jeter and Juelke 1978), rival the best Persian and Turkish rugs in intricacy, quality, and price. Most rugs made in Teotitlán fall in terms of difficulty and sophistication between the Hernández boys' apprentice efforts and Mendoza's tour de force. Nevertheless the entire genre exhibits all the kinds of intensification found in modern crafts, that is, the same matrix of change illustrated by the pillowcase discussed in chapter 1 (figures 5–6).

Intensification through selection is the rarest type in this craft, though present especially in choices of dyes. The birds-and-flowers rug by the de los Angeles family uses no dyes, just the various colors of un-dyed natural wool. Most family studios offer only one or two of these rugs at a time, displaying them for their special, romantically weighted effect. Slightly more common are rugs with just a few colors or varia-tions on one—we own one almost completely woven in shades of red, all from cochineal. Intensification through virtuosity marks the overall improvement of weaving technique in the craft, with that rising stan-dard caused by increasingly careful training and by competition, with a few star craftsmen doing especially tight weaves. Also, certain sophisti-cated designs evince intellectual virtuosity—this is present in both the Hernández boys' delightful small rugs and Arnulfo Mendoza's master-work. But the dominant trend in design intensification here over the last few decades is through addition, whether that be within a rug (add-ing colors or design elements or shrinking the size of elements to make room for more) or within the tradition as a whole (adding numbers of designs, etc., as weavers seek simultaneously to carve out niches and to capture the attention of every potential customer).

### The Sociology of the Rug Trade in Teotitlán del Valle

The makers of the rugs pictured in this book represent several broad trends in how the craft is pursued and marketed. These topics over-lap: geography, gender, the training of weavers, and the intricate psy-chology and practice of national and international sales. Even the least skilled and most modestly successful weavers in Teotitlán create rugs worth studying and considering for purchase. Families who have neither outstanding skill nor geographic advantage (that is, their family home-studio is not on a main street frequented by tourists in Teotitlán, and they do not rent a stall in any market) may sell through middlemen in Teotitlán or Oaxaca city. Alternatively they may try to neutralize the negative effect of poor location by sending some member of the family out to troll for customers. In the most common form of this ubiquitous practice, older family members stroll the village's main streets and invite tourists to come with them to see their family's output. There are many variations on this technique. For instance, the driver of the taxi shuttle from the Pan-American Highway to downtown Teotitlán offers to take tourists to what he asserts is the best rug studio and store in the city, one coincidentally owned by his family (one of their fine rugs is now in our front entryway). And it is easy to hitchhike from the highway into the center of Teotitlán or its neighbor Santa Ana if one doesn't mind visiting the home-studio of the family of the driver. On the other end of the scale, the most successful weavers have developed international contacts and ship many or most of their rugs abroad.

Most of Teotitlán's weaving families pursue several sales strategies at once. The de los Angeles family, whose home-studio is on a main street, sells a good half of their rugs through a carefully developed handful of international contacts but nevertheless maintains a stall many Saturdays at the large public Mercado de Abastos in Oaxaca—that is where I first met José and two of his sons. The Mendoza family, whose work is shown in figure 14, can rely mostly on their home-studio's excellent location on a main street (just four blocks toward the center on the same street as the de los Angeles home, but drawing on about four times as much tourist foot traffic). However, they also participate in the Saturday market in Oaxaca.

The most elaborate combination of sales strategies I encountered is the one pursued by Felipe Hernández (see figure 18), whose home-studio is at a disadvantageous distance from any tourist corridor in the village. Felipe drives to Oaxaca, hangs around on the main square for an hour or two most afternoons, gently and cleverly initiates conversations with tourists, and eventually works those chats around to the possibility of visiting Teotitlán and seeing his rugs while there. He is a charming and knowledgeable companion and became a main contact in Teotitlán for both Andra Stanton (the psychiatric social worker whose passion for crafts led her to open a store in Massachusetts and to write the best book on Oaxaca rugs) and for me.

I was sitting on a bench on Oaxaca's square one afternoon in May 1995. A Zapotec man about thirty years old, who turned out to be Felipe, sat down at the other end of the bench and studied an English textbook intently for a few minutes. He asked for my help after a while, but this was a pretext for chatting about Oaxaca (in English that turned out to be deliberate in pace but precise and grammatical) and about his home of Teotitlán, which he offered to show to me, my wife, and our little daughter. We consented and took him to lunch at the one very nice restaurant in the village (in part to be friendly, but also partly to avoid incurring a possible obligation through accepting his strategic hospitality). He did show us his home and workshop, and rugs for sale as the climax of the tour. He was visibly disappointed but still gracious when we bought nothing on that first visit.

I continued to run into Felipe on or near the square during each subsequent trip to Oaxaca. In time, he was sharing a small shop on a side street in a good mercantile section of Oaxaca with a partner representing a family of *alebrije* (demon) makers. By 2002 he was renting an upgraded shop with the same partner on Alcalá, the tourist pedestrian street running north from the square. At that time he was still trolling (for rug customers, and also as a tour guide), had one steady customer in the United States (Stanton, who commissioned specific designs), and also sold through a cooperative in Sedona, Arizona, which is a center for marketing Navajo crafts. He had a bed-and-breakfast planned as part of a new home being built slowly in Teotitlán. Nevertheless he continued to get up every morning at 4 a.m. to weave for several hours, an activity with which he also ended his varied and busy days. It seemed like a success story to me, but he regarded his improved status as fragile; he considered the eclecticism of his pursuits as the best strategy to guard against unpredictable setbacks.

My other most regular contact in Teotitlán is Isabel Gutierrez, whom I always encounter where I met her, at her family's stall in the small rug market in the center of the village (figures 19 and 32). Like many weavers, she began her apprenticeship when she was around six. Although she progressed well as a craftsman, she assumed her current job as main seller for the extended family when the downtown market was founded in the mid-1980s, and has worked there since. Each morning, she is weaving by 6 a.m., then in place at the market by 9 a.m. or so. She goes home at about 6 p.m. and weaves for another hour in the evening. Those who weave fewer hours accumulate less skill and so are assigned easier design types. Isabel, with only three or four hours of weaving time a day, sticks to simple geometric figures. Indeed, women tend to weave less-taxing designs than do men, though they certainly do weave, despite the treadle loom having been the province of men historically. Gender roles persist strongly in the most generic tasks—men farm, women cook and clean—but in the exercise of a village's main craft, these roles flex, becoming guidelines rather than rigid doctrine. Within the series of processes associated with rug making, women do somewhat more in the areas of dyeing yarn and assembling skeins of yarn and generally spend more time on chores unrelated to weaving. In the Mendoza family, the men weave an average of nine hours per day, whereas the women average about six hours, a typical contrast. Also typically, the women weave relatively simple patterns. Several women who are the designated sellers for their extended families told me this, and some of these women added that designs including curves were reserved for certain men in their families.

Weaving assignments also correlate with generation to a considerable extent. As in the Hernández family, children pass through an initial stage during which they make small rugs that feature straightforward geometric figures, thus minimizing the visibility of loose or unevenly tight weaving, which can result in rugs not having straight sides. The chair-seat-sized weavings shown in figure 1 were made by Felipe Hernández's sons Victor (the rug on the left) and Erick (the one on the right), in both cases when the weaver was about ten years old. I also bought a few of the boys' tiny weavings that we use as drink coasters. There is a substantial and stable market for small weavings; the fruits of apprenticeship smoothly take their place in family finances.

Older weavers in many families also make relatively simple designs because they learned to weave when the town was still building a market for rugs and the designs were simpler on average than they are today. Most of the men who did the weaving then still devoted much of their day to farming. But all of this works well in the marketplace, since certain groups of tourists prefer geometric designs.

### Wood Carvings in San Antonio Arrazola and San Martín Tilcajete

The second most famous distinctly Oaxacan craft, and the one with the least historical continuity, is the carving and painting of wooden animals, monsters, angels, and other figurines. I will be able to discuss this craft more quickly, since it parallels weaving and pottery in many ways. San Antonio Arrazola, where the modern practice started, is about twenty kilometers from Oaxaca in the shadow of the ruins of Monte Albán. One travels most easily to Arrazola by collective taxi. San Martín Tilcajete is a little farther away, off the highway to Ocotlán, reachable by bus to the crossroads (and walking in or taking a shuttle). One most easily returns by *colectivo* to Ocotlán and then either bus or colectivo to Oaxaca. La Unión Tejalapam is about as near to Oaxaca but is harder to get to, involving fording a creek or two; other villages venturing into the craft are farther up into the mountains (notably Ejutla, above Mitla). Just Arrazola and San Martín are visited by lots of tourists; the other towns sell their wares primarily though Oaxacan and international middlemen (which is also part of the eclectic sales strategies of even the most famous carvers in Arrazola and San Martín, just as it is for the top weavers in Teotitlán).

Craftspersons have carved masks and toys for centuries in Oaxaca. Moving from the whittling of toys for children to a widespread practice of making cunningly conceived and highly decorated wooden animals, fanciful figures, and religious icons was initiated by one crabby, egotistical individualist, Manuel Jiménez of Arrazola (b. 1919). He was originally a hard-drinking jack-of-all-trades. His eccentric hobby of making strikingly elaborate wooden figures was noticed and encouraged by an American resident in Oaxaca, Arthur Train, in the late 1950s. Train sparked a modest American enthusiasm for Jiménez's work, and the Mexican depression (coupled with American prosperity) in the mid-1980s caused the market to expand suddenly. Nearly all the carvers in all the villages now dedicated to this craft began after 1985 (Barbash and Ragan 1993, 14). The timing of the rupture in the function and in the practice of the craft and the later wide expansion of it matches well with those milestones in the histories of black pottery, of rug weaving, and, for that matter, most of the crafts of Oaxaca and elsewhere in Mexico. This is significant: this synchronizing reflects that the major changes respond to overriding socioeconomic factors more than to any rhythms in tradition itself. Indeed, while San Bartolo's black pottery and Teotitlán's rugs mutated out of venerable but dying professions in those villages, the carvings issued from a hobby no more cultivated in the eventual wood-carving villages than it had been pursued elsewhere in Mexico.

In my discussion of wood carving, I refer to the following photographs:

Figure 2. Carvings by María Jiménez Ojeda and her brothers Arón and Roman of San Martín Tilcajete.

Figure 20. An array of carvings by Antonio Mardarin of Arrazola.

Figure 21. A variety of carvings: a deer probably from La Unión (rather old-fashioned, with aniline paint); a fairly crude alebrije (demon), probably from Arrazola; and a tuba-carrying toucan by Martín Melchor Angeles of San Martín.

Figure 22. María Jiménez Ojeda, standing behind a commissioned large religious piece.

Figure 23. Mary Jane Gagnier de Mendoza, in front of a tapestry woven by her husband, Arnulfo Mendoza, holding a wooden yak made by Luis Pablo Mendoza (no relation).

Manuel Jiménez's early carvings already explored a wide subject matter. He and his sons "are best known for their animals, angels, shepherds, kings and Christ figures" (Rothstein and Rothstein 2002, 86). This set the course for the incredible modern proliferation of designs of animals (actual and imagined, natural and anthropomorphic) and dream figures (religious and demonic, fleshed and skeletal, plus monsters, like the alebrije at the center of figure 21). The history of making these carvings for tourists—a short history, but one exhibiting clear trends—is marked by hyperbolically increasing sophistication in conception and execution. Early aniline paint, which tended to soak into the wood (see the unsigned deer on the left in figure 21), yielded quickly to the use of vivid tints of house paints, just as simple dots and lines gave way to elaborate patterns. Of course, as craft families constantly seek distinctive market niches, one path is to look back—hence that deer, a rustic, deliberately simple example—and the yak in figure 23, a smooth and modern yet deliberately spare piece of art, an example of intensification by selection.[2] Sizes moved from medium to small and truly miniature. Today all sizes are available, still concentrating on small, easily packed (and easily displayed) pieces, but punctuated by the occasional large, expensive piece, such as María Jiménez Ojeda's extravagant carving of the Mother Mary

Figure 20. Antonio Mardarin of Arrazola created this rich array of carvings. Most craft families try to balance serving established tastes and attracting special notice by supplementing bread-and-butter carvings with something unusual; I saw some, but not many, carvings of the Virgin of Guadalupe elsewhere in Arrazola.

Figure 21. A variety of carvings: a deer probably from La Unión (rather old-fashioned, finished with aniline paint), a fairly crude alebrije (demon), probably from Arrazola, and a tuba-playing toucan by Martín Melchor Angeles of San Martín Tilcajete. His 1997 business card mentioned the specialties of animal bicyclists, animal fishermen, and chairs. That year, occasionally having two beasts per bicycle was new, as was attaching a sidecar.

and the angelic host (figure 22), commissioned by an affluent American woman for her husband on the occasion of their twenty-fifth anniversary.

Many men in the carving villages still farm part-time, despite the poor quality and limited amount of land, and women remain responsible for all their traditional domestic duties. But just as in the cases of all other crafts, gender assignments bend in this new pursuit. Men have the primary assignment of carving and sanding, and women the initial role of painting, but the division of labor flexes depending on how long tasks take and on gender ratios within families. A few women do carve, and most men end up helping paint. Indeed, while a majority of pieces are signed by the men in this collaboration, in cases where the painting sets the pieces apart, the tourist market has demanded that the painter do the signing, whether male or female.

The carved animals in figure 2 exemplify several trends in this craft. They are made by the Jiménez Ojeda family of San Martín Tilcajete, with the dog and elephant signed by María, and the turtle and pig signed

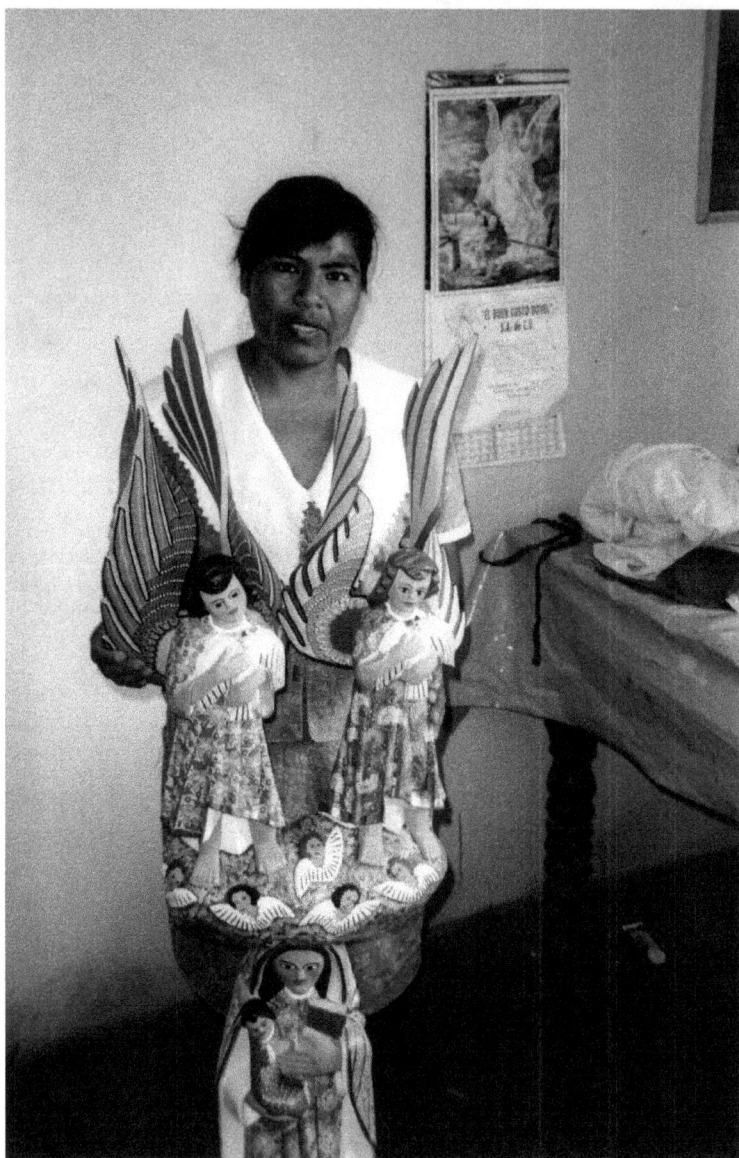

Figure 22. María Jiménez Ojeda, standing behind her incredibly extravagant carved and painted depiction of the Mother Mary and the angelic host (commissioned by a American woman for her husband on the occasion of their twenty-fifth anniversary) in her home in San Martín Tilcajete, 1998.

Figure 23. Mary Jane Gagnier de Mendoza, in front of a silk tapestry by her husband Arnulfo Mendoza, in their store, Mano Magíca, the highest-end crafts outlet in Oaxaca. She is holding a wooden yak by Luis Pablo Mendoza (no relation).

by her younger brothers Roman and Arón, respectively. As throughout the wood-carving villages (and the rug and pottery villages), the families work together. The men carve in the outdoor courtyard, and the painting is done by everyone, either at tables in the shade or in rooms with windows that open onto the courtyard. It is work done individually. Each craftsperson labors alone—that is, just one person works on a particular carving at a given moment—yet collaboratively (for example, María paints what her brothers carved), and normally in a group setting. Figure 2 illustrates the routine tension between tradition and practicality in gender roles in that all the carving is done by the men (women do this rarely, and only in families lacking or very short on males), but the men paint, too, since the overriding goal is to crank out as many finished pieces as possible.

Today the best work is virtuosic indeed. Since the conspicuous (and salable) excellence here is in the painting, María signs the work she paints, and the men take pains to say they work following her models. Why did she choose flowers as her dominant decorating element, as shown in figure 2? She embroidered to earn money until she was about twenty; it would have been natural to carry some of the elegant patterns from one craft to the other (see Rothstein and Rothstein 2002, 101–2; flowers are the signature element in most Oaxacan embroidery). But Barbash reports that María told him her shift early in her painting career from decorating just with little dots to employing flowers happened as follows: "One morning we went out into the fields. It was a beautiful day, barely raining. The desert looks wonderful in the rain. There were flowers, green leaves, yellow stalks, so many colors. And I asked myself, 'How can I do it like this? How can I paint like this?' That's how it started. That's how we all start probably—by seeing the beauty around us" (1993, 66). However, in relating a version of this oft-repeated story to me on several occasions, she described the images of flower, birds, and butterflies coming to her "in a dream." I have found that southern Mexican Indians are loath to cite individual creativity as artistic impetus, instead claiming repeatedly that ideas arrive "in dreams," thus channeled through a spiritual source outside of them. María's flowers probably arrived on the scene by a combination of these paths, the same means that her colleagues in the village draw on: nature, inspiration, and cross-fertilization from other crafts.

María's concentration on flowers (and her brothers' use of similar-sized elements from nature) also illustrates both niche seeking and hectic innovation in the carving business. She also specializes in the large winged angels that she designs, Arón carves, and she paints, as in figure 22. Other carving families specialize in cats, armadillos, trains, perky owls, and others, or decorate with curved lines or with amoeba-like designs, and so on. Martín Melchor Angeles and his wife and daughter often carve music ensembles made up of devils. He likes bands in general—I've purchased a drumming zebra and toucan tuba player from him (figure 21)—but his signature product is animals bicycling. I purchased a spotted dog on a bike in 1995. In 1997 he pointed out that he had some carvings with two animals per bicycle, and a few with a sidecar attached. The better carvers constantly add something new to their repertoires to avoid boredom, to satisfy foreign wholesalers who swoop down semiannually in their SUVs, and to open the wallets of collectors. Indeed, just as in the rug villages, even the top craftsmen here insist on pursuing multiple sales strategies. For instance, María and her brothers sell to international dealers and through at least two middlemen in Oaxaca (one being the gallery Mano Mágica), but also to individuals who pass by. I've been grateful—and a little surprised—when, on several occasions, members of this highly successful craft family chose to hustle to finish a piece for me while I waited.

María's flowers also represent a particular kind of intensification through addition, in which two-dimensional figural elements adorn sculptures, providing both a secondary layer for visual focus and, in these cases, a depicted environment that the carving carries with them. Her dog and elephant both inhabit the outdoors, but each has one element beyond the botanical. The elephant has birds on it, too—many of María's decorative schemes supplement flowers with birds or butterflies. The dog's poinsettias are seasonal: I bought this during the Christmas season, and she did volunteer that it was a Christmas dog. Her brothers' animals incorporate botanical and zoological design elements, too. The turtle, whose head and limbs received camouflage patterns, has fish on its back, and the pig is either imbued with essence of pig through being decorated with his fellow pigs, or is being shown as many pigs live, surrounded in close quarters by other swine.

Last, I would argue that this array of animals illustrates the concentric geographic rings surrounding these craftsmen. Pigs are domestic, turtles are wild but local, and good-looking, healthy dogs are creatures of the middle or upper class or points north in Mexico (village dogs are composed mostly of ribs and fleas). The elephant represents animals never seen in person by locals—much-thumbed copies of *National Geographic* circulate in the village (religious objects represent distance in another way). This is much the same journey of subject matter portrayed in the design elements of rugs, which feature grecas and crosses (which are local, from ruins within twenty kilometers of Teotitlán), pan-Mexican ancient images from clay stamps and codices, Saltillo diamonds, Navajo motifs from yet farther away, and, from the most distant source of ideas, European paintings. The selection of subjects by the carvers and by the weavers represents parallel journeys of imagination.

I now broaden this summary with a pair of tables juxtaposing the Chiapas pillowcase discussed in chapter 1 with the Oaxacan crafts of black pottery, rugs, and carvings. Table 1 concerns broad matters of historical understanding. Each craft is not a relic of earlier times but a product of a "rupture," an embodiment of recent change that responds to changing history and to the emotional needs (and mercantile willingness) of outsiders. However, each maintains two kinds of links with the past. One link is in the craft articles themselves, visual elements that represent historical continuity or a "classical" school within the riot of variety in the modern craft. The other link is in explanation or demonstration: you know these are authentic handmade crafts because you can travel to the villages and *see* such crafts being handmade.

Table 2 concerns the element of folkloric intensification and needs little further explanation. When historic crafts are recast, even reborn as souvenirs, and cultural rupture takes place through crafts' separation from historic functions, the consequent diminishing of total meaning is attenuated by adding visual elements, and craft tilts toward art.

I close the chapter by revisiting craftspersons' motives. I explored the subject of motive most thoroughly in interviews in connection with

| Table 1 | Crafts Summary 1: Crafts in History | | |
|---|---|---|---|
| Craft Object or Genre | Nature of Rupture in Meaning or Function | Historicism/ Classicism | Explanation/ Demonstration/ Contextualization |
| Pillowcase from San Cristóbal de las Casas | Designs bearing religious or community significance become just decoration; go from huipil to sampler | Design "ancestors" is typical size; use as border unsurprising; backstrap loom tech. | Store manager can explain; context provided by city outside, not in store |
| Black pottery from San Bartolo Coyotepec | Large gray pots to carry mescal or water became smaller black pots, no longer watertight | Weak: a few modern small pots look like the earlier large pots; large pots on display | Son of inventor of black pottery gives demonstrations in condensed form |
| Rugs from Teotitlán del Valle and Santa Ana del Valle | Serapes became rugs, many of which in turn became wall hangings or purses, pillowcases, etc. | Many rugs are same size and technique as serapes; many historical designs used | Looms on display; demonstration is part of sales pitch; may show cactus |
| Carvings from Arrazola and San Martín Tilcajete | Toys for local children (rough, expendable, replaceable, larger) became adults' decorator accents | Weak: a very few carved animals are deliberately rustic and simple | Carving and painting going on constantly in courtyard, etc., where alebrijes sold |

weaving, but the themes that emerged hold for the carving and pottery towns, too. The question "why do you and your family weave?" provoked two sets of responses. One array of replies seemed rehearsed: *Weaving was traditional in the town. Doing it maintained connections with local and family history, and felt authentic. It was the right thing to do.* I heard this several times, with many phrases recurring nearly identically. It seemed like a memorate that, truly believed or not, had become central to the sales process. On the other hand, interviewees like the Mendozas spoke of *keeping the family together (that is, maintaining a clan economy that didn't require anyone to migrate north for work) and supporting better educational opportunities for younger members of the family.* Here the continuity of profession supported a more general pair of traditions, that of family life and of wanting good things for the

| Table 2   Crafts Summary 2: Types of Intensification in Modern Cafts | | | |
|---|---|---|---|
| Craft Object or Genre | Intensification through Addition | Intensification through Selection | Intensification through Virtuosity |
| Pillowcase from San Cristóbal de las Casas | Not featured here, but found in many huipiles and other objects for tourists | A customary 6–10 colors thinned to just 3 here, though the dark purple is extremely rich | Above-average work in weaving both the central panel and background fabric |
| Black pottery from San Bartolo Coyotepec | Focused especially on design elements such as cutouts, gold leaf, and rare colors | Pottery remains black, and individual pieces add just a few colors or other special features | Pots are more regular in shape than in the past and require more skill for intricate effects |
| Rugs from Teotitlán del Valle | More colors and elements per rug; denser designs; proliferation of designs | Using no dyes (just the natural wool colors) or few; selecting a single design for a given rug | Better, tighter weaving; exceptional balance of design elements; doing own unique designs |
| Carvings from Arrazola and San Martín Tilcajete | A constant factor: more and denser designs on wilder choices of figures | Not very significant; a few carvings have scaled-back numbers of colors; more natural | Constantly smoother carving and sanding; Denser painted designs require precise painting |

young. Felipe Hernández carefully integrated helping his sons into his daily routine. He found enough money to send them to private high school in Oaxaca; they rode into town on the bus, and he drove them home each afternoon after trolling for customers on the square. His oldest son, Victor, followed Felipe into the weaving business, as did Victor's wife. Jorge parlayed the English he learned in this school into occasional employment in the United States (sometimes as family representative, other times on his own), and the youngest, Erick, studied mechanical engineering.

In the Hernández family, we see the broad stance of the village of Teotitlán in miniature, indeed, the collective attitude prevalent in all the craft villages: don't let the next generation lose touch with the village's reliable occupation and the economic foundation of one's family, but consider replacing the historic supplement to weaving (or throwing pots, etc.)—that is, farming—with more lucrative and enjoyable professions that can be pursued locally, such as teaching, mechanics, administration, even medicine. Nevertheless the broad principle of having some family members pursue supplementary occupations persists. No matter how lucrative a given craft becomes, villagers stubbornly resist putting all their eggs in one basket in the sphere of employment. This reluctance—on the surface more than a little inefficient—parallels the one that inspires their multiple sales strategies (that is, craftspeople will accommodate individual customers like me on the spot even when doing so delays work on craft items that have been commissioned by international buyers who may in fact pay more).

Whether craftspeople claim a genre of crafts is old, such as the rugs and pottery, or cheerfully admit it is young, such as the carvings, and although making those crafts meshes nicely with inherited psychology, *all* the populations of current *customers* are new. The residents of the major craft villages know that outsiders' tastes can be fickle and that local and national political volatility can affect the tourist trade adversely. Shifting economic sands are part of local history; acting calmly and gracefully in the face of the continuity of insecurity is yet another facet of local tradition. Also, the successful craftspersons of the central valleys must be keenly aware that most other rural citizens of Oaxaca do not share their good fortune but are instead stuck in an economy based on subsistence agriculture, a situation that is less and less tenable. The economic, social, and psychological blessings attendant on family-based craft businesses are welcomed, but not fully trusted.

# 3.

# Tradition and Tourism in Festival Life: Shaping and Marketing Oaxaca's Guelaguetza

On two Mondays each July, the indigenous populations of the state of Oaxaca collaborate with the state tourist board and various cultural organizations to present the country's most spectacular festival, the Guelaguetza. A dozen or more dance troupes from all over the state, accompanied by either their own small band or the state brass band—a total of about five hundred dancers and musicians—perform for an audience of over twelve thousand in an open-air hillside venue built for the festival overlooking the city of Oaxaca. Many thousands more watch on television, and the two sessions of dance and music on the hill combine with dozens of linked events in the city to create a complex and continuous fortnight of fiesta. The total event has become massive and equally intricate as both aesthetic and political statement.

Without tourist money, no festival this large would be possible. The Guelaguetza is the highest point in Oaxaca's tourist calendar and thus the annual focus for the local economy (the other, lesser high seasons being the weeks surrounding Christmas and the Day of the Dead). A broad partnership, the Guelaguetza depends on several population groups being happy with the composite event beyond its aesthetic qualities. Tourists satisfy a generalized nostalgia by considering the Guelaguetza an authentic representation of valuable aspects of an equally generalized past, the powerful of Oaxaca reassert their comfortable position at the state's socioeconomic pinnacle, and the dancers and musicians welcome both the opportunity to see their indigenous identity celebrated publicly and a free trip to the big city.

Many people who live in metropolitan Oaxaca enjoy the festivities and the immediate economic benefits of tourist dollars. But many others harbor serious reservations about the event as a political and economic statement. In this chapter, I examine the Guelaguetza through 2005, and in the final chapter I touch on more recent developments.

The broad outline of the symbiosis between event, government, outsider audience, and local populace is straightforward. It costs plenty to put on the festival. Participants in the Guelaguetza are not paid beyond food, lodging, and transportation, but there are lots of them—I conservatively estimate five hundred because there are an average of twenty troupes overall, each filling a bus (twelve or more troupes per Monday, with some overlap between the ensembles dancing the two days). And security involves many more bodies than does the entertainment. Police and temporary armed guards are hired liberally both because of the sheer size of the event and because it attracts some extremely high-profile visitors (one estimate for numbers of employees given in 2002 included 1,123 police, 80 cleaners, and over 200 legal vendors; see Chavela Rivas 2002). After all, every socioeconomic level is represented liberally in the audience, packed more tightly together than in daily life, with the potential for friction. Hundreds of state employees help the city prepare for the onslaught of visitors. The money must come from somewhere. The local elite supplement their own funds—although affluent, they are not numerous—by looking to points north in Mexico and also abroad, to American and a few European tourists. In 2002 the Secretary of Tourism (Secretario de Desarollo Turistico, commonly called Sedetur) estimated that for every peso invested by the state, precisely 56.55 were earned, for a total of (less precisely, but grandly estimated) some five billion pesos (Chavela Rivas 2002).

I attended my first Guelaguetza in 1995. The event saturated the newspapers, hotel prices rose, and taxi drivers charged more than usual. Oaxaca was clearly in high gear. The basic publicity campaign formed a litany echoed in newspapers, speeches, and flyers and placards distributed by the tourist office, broadcasting a formula that all visitors can soon easily internalize: "Guelaguetza" is a Zapotec word that means sharing generously.[1] Some sort of ceremony centered on this theme has been going on for a long, long time. The current Guelaguetza began in 1932, and colorful troupes of "Indians" from the "seven regions" of the state are delighted to dance for an audience now. Information presented and repeated in this way constitutes what anthropologists and folklorists call "memorates," stories told so many times that not just broad outlines but also intimate details of vocabulary have crystallized. But here the memorate belongs not to a storyteller or two but to the media, including flyers distributed at the tourist offices. A modest amount of additional detail appears in scholarly work (e.g., Acevedo Conde), but this more academic fleshing out of the media's memorate is not readily available to tourists or to the general public unless they pursue research in a library. I will supplement the public memorate here: The event had the official title of Lunes del Cerro (Mondays on the Hill) until 1951, when the more ethnic word "Guelaguetza" was added. The two titles are used interchangeably or in tandem today. The auditorium on the hill was completed in 1974 and was designed to hold an audience of 11,400; up to about 15,000 have often crowded into that space.

During each of the two Mondays, audience members arrive by taxi, city bus, tour bus, or foot. For the pedestrians—the less-affluent attendees—it is an easy stroll from downtown for twenty minutes or so, then quite a climb up hundreds of broad steps flanked by dozens of temporary market stands and food stands. Modest lines for the elite paid seats end with the same thorough search by machine-gun-toting teenage security guards that greets people enduring the longer lines leading to the free seats.

The stage looks out over the city, with concrete stadium-style arcs of seats reaching far up the contour of the hill. The audience faces downhill. Thus, as one watches the dancers, one also sees the band behind them, with the city distant and far below as a backdrop, with the perpetual haze obscuring differences between rich and poor neighborhoods. The about 2,400 seats close to the stage run about $30 to $50 for guaranteed spots. The free seats—about ten thousand of them—are first come, first served. A barrier and armed security separate the few expensively dressed folks in the inner arcs from the enormous crowds behind. This dichotomy reflects the fact that until recently there was a straightforward division of Mexican citizens into a tiny upper class and enormous much, much lower class. However, the two thousand ticketed seats constitute a far greater fraction of the whole than is justified by the tiny ratio of upper- to lower-class citizens, so tourists *must* enter the picture to fill most of those expensive seats.

Another process of "filling in" the festivities may catch foreign tourists off guard. Many public events in Mexico are free. Worthwhile free events are packed hours ahead of publicized start times. Over the years, authorities have found that it's considerate—and a simple way to keep crowds peaceful—to supplement the show with warm-up acts starting an hour or more ahead of the advertised event. I arrived at my first Guelaguetza at 8:20 a.m., a theoretical hour and forty minutes early. Few of the paid seats were occupied yet, but I was glad I'd purchased one, because the more than ten thousand free seats behind me were already full. Ten minutes after I sat down, *chirimías* played, then the state marimba ensemble, and so on through announcements, grandly declaimed romantic poems, and endless patriotic rhetoric right up to the formal program, which finally commenced precisely when advertised. It must start on time every time, since it is televised live.

The Guelaguetza itself opens with a newly crowned "corn goddess" walking around the stage to wild applause (more about her later). There is a separate box for a dozen or so special guests at the back of the paying section, and a walkway directly from the stage to the exclusive box that performers traverse to pay homage to the rulers of Oaxaca. In 1995 a typical array of high-status guests (the first lady of Mexico, several state governors, sports stars, and other rich individuals) were joined by Lupita Jones, the Mexican Miss Universe 1991. A multilayered encounter indeed: Miss Universe, heir to ancient pagan harvest rituals, meeting the eyes of the corn goddess, just crowned in a ceremony structured much like a modern beauty pageant. Another year, the state governor was "spontaneously" convinced to come down and waltz with a lissome young dancer (his security guards moved into a revised formation ahead of time—they had this "surprise" tightly choreographed on and off the stage).

Now to the main event, when all present are in one or another tourist mode. Twelve to fifteen dance troupes dance for a total elapsed time of three to three and a half hours: a long time to sit and pay attention, since it's hot. Each troupe owns a slot of around fifteen minutes during which they march onstage, perform a medley of truncated dances or other act of appropriate length, then enthusiastically throw offerings into the crowd: Guelaguetza means sharing, we are reminded by the emcee as we do our best to catch our share of projectile offerings, which range from fruit or little loaves of bread to small baskets or other crafts. One of the advantages of the reserved, paid-for seats is that you may get to take some of these offerings home: just a few aerodynamic limes thrown by athletic young male dancers reach the free seats. On my first visit, I caught some rock-hard braided bread and a mango, then was blindsided by a pineapple that someone else wrestled away. Other years I have trekked very early to the free seats, which are rowdy conflations of locals and budget tourists (a busload of retired electricians from Monterrey sat behind me once). One Monday in 2002 I was adopted into a family group run by a young Zapotec woman. She performed the miracle of getting her relatives (and me) into contiguous areas in the stands, efficiently delegating responsibilities: "Save those three seats, Cristóbal [me]; Isabel will bring you a drink." We affluent visitors are asked to believe that all of Oaxaca is delighted with the event, and in the auditorium during those three or so hours, there is no evidence to the contrary. Even the poorest of the folks in the free seats are in fiesta mode, socializing, snacking constantly, and even watching the distant stage sporadically.

The mornings of dance are carefully shaped, with the different troupes' contributions ordered to yield a strong show. Each ensemble's short appearance is standardized in certain ways. All groups march on when announced, then dance, with gender- specific or gender-alternating lines dissolving frequently into twirling couples. Initial short sections of dance performed to music sounding like polkas or waltzes eventually yield to quicker ones, with more foot stomping in prescribed patterns as the music shifts to *sones* and *jarabes* (in a brisk 6/8 or in that superimposing of 6/8 and 3/4 called sesquialtera). After the dance and music climax, the dancers throw their offerings to the crowd. Beyond that general framework, each group must be special, or there would be little point to having many troupes. Each ensemble constitutes a group of models showing off region-specific festive clothes. The men usually wear white outfits (hat colors can vary, as can the occasional addition of blankets and other region-specific accessories). The women's dance outfits adventurously explore variations within regional patterns. For instance, if skirts worn by women in a given ensemble are in solid colors with black lateral stripes, these many different solid colors create contrast (though remaining of parallel intensity).

Each ensemble offers its own array of dance formations within the basic line dance environment, that is, certain groupings of couples, or a solo couple surrounded by the group, or straight lines or circles, or various kaleidoscopic realignments. Some groups content themselves with modified line dances, while others incorporate contrasting visual or procedural special features. Stylized attempts to steal kisses are quite common, as are mock bullfights. In other cases, one dancer carries a turkey (hobbled and alive) or a papier-mâché swordfish, or garlands of greens, or a bottle (in one fairly common dance in which a man pretends to be drunk). Further contrasts concern musical features. A troupe may bring its own band or rely on the Oaxaca state band (which leaves more room for dancers on the bus the state furnishes to bring them from their homes to the city of Oaxaca). If they employ their own band, it may be a typical village brass band or, less likely, a more antiquated string-based group. Several troupes always perform a famous waltz song associated with their respective homes, and one features salty exchanges of quips between men and women of courting age and bent. And the particular mix of sections of music metered and paced like marches, polkas, waltzes, and sones is also idiosyncratic.

### Four Dances from the 2007 Guelaguetza

To sample the approaches pursued by various dance troupes, I include four photographs of the "delegations" that performed at the first Guelaguetza of 2007 (figures 24–27). The delegations were from, respectively, Santa María Asunción Tlaxiaco, also known as the Heroica Ciudad (Heroic City) of Tlaxiaco (following local practice for abbreviating city titles, I'll just call it Tlaxiaco), San Juan Bautista Tuxtepec (henceforth Tuxtepec), San Antonino Castillo Velasco (henceforth San

Figure 24. Performing in the first Guelaguetza of 2007 (two take place during July, on successive Mondays; starting in 2005 there have been two on each Monday), the dance troupe from Santa María Asunción Tlaxiaco, also known as the Heroica Ciudad (Heroic City) of Tlaxiaco.

Figure 25. In the 2007 Guelaguetza, the dance troupe from San Juan Bautista Tuxtepec.

Figure 26. In the 2007 Guelaguetza, the dance troupe from San Antonino Castillo Velasco.

Figure 27. In the 2007 Guelaguetza, the dance troupe from San Pedro Ixcatlán. The three cities whose dancers appear in figures 24–26 contribute dance troupes to the Guelaguetza every year, but Ixcatlán was a new participant in 2007.

Antonino), and San Pedro Ixcatlán (henceforth Ixcatlán). The first three cities contribute dance troupes to the Guelaguetza every year, but Ixcatlán was a new participant in 2007.

Tlaxiaco is located 180 kilometers northeast of Oaxaca, at about 2,040 meters above sea level, in a small valley surrounded by conifer-covered mountains within the region of the state called the Mixteca. It is in touch with national trends—the highway between the big cities of Puebla and Veracruz passes through—and is the mercantile and population center for the Mixteca Alta, the higher part of the Mixteca region. Its weekly market is second in size only to that of Oaxaca itself. The vast majority of residents are ethnically Mixtec (there are some Triqui[2] present also), though only some 9,399 of 34,587 residents counted in the 2005 census speak an indigenous language. Just under a quarter of workers grow crops, while another quarter work in some part of the timber industry, and the remaining half work in the service sector.[3] Employment isn't low by Mexican standards, and tourism makes some mark on the local economy. Nevertheless, some 30 percent of workers have to migrate north for employment most years. That points up one reason the Guelaguetza matters to the municipalities that contribute dance troupes: just as in the craft villages discussed in the previous chapter, these areas hope through the exposure of the festival to attract more tourists and thus be able to employ more of their men at home, strengthening community and family life.

When the dancers from Tlaxiaco parade onto the stage, their own band plays one of the most famous songs in the Spanish language, "Canción Mixteca" (figure 24). A Mixtec Indian named José López Alevés wrote this song in 1912 in Mexico City, where he had gone to study at the National Conservatory. It's a song full of nostalgia, a waltz in the genre of a ranchera (meaning a rural song about love, here love primarily for the home left behind). After we hear those poignant strains for about five minutes, and most members of the audience have waved their hats back and forth in the customary accompaniment to this hit (as have the male dancers), a female dancer gives a speech in Mixtec, and her partner relays the speech in Spanish (the speech turns out to be the sort introducing every dance, one praising the dancers' home in considerable detail). Then the troupe embarks on a series of excerpts, each about a minute long, from local traditional dances, as follows:

"Son de Fiesta," in a quick 6/8 time, with the dancers still marching, and sombreros still waving;

"Jarabe Inicial," a son in a slow sesquialtera, with the dancers in two lines;

"La Petenera" (a genre alternating measures in 3/4 and 6/8, like Leonard Bernstein's "America" from West Side Story) in a minor key, during which men wave red handkerchiefs;

"El Panadero" (The Baker), another son with the dancers facing in lines (the photo came from this sequence);

"El Toro," in march time; the men pretend to be bulls and the woman matadors;

"La Vaca," in 6/8; roles reversed;

"El Borracho" (The Drunkard), in 3/4, a couple dance that in many versions has a man explicitly miming inebriation (by weaving and falling down), but not in this version;

"La Sarna" (Mange), in a quicker 3/4; men scratch women;

"Los Enanos" (The Dwarfs); in the same quick 3/4, with dancers hopping up repeatedly from very low crouches as they proceed around the stage;

"Jarabe Final," a slow son like the "Jarabe Inicial";

and to march off, a reprise of the "Son de Fiesta," with the men waving their hats again.

These eleven excerpts fit into ten minutes, so that the entire performance fits into the requisite fifteen-minute slot. The whole package constitutes a typical sampler approach to a community's contribution; the reader will recognize many of the ingredients from the preceding general characterization of Guelaguetza dance acts.

Figure 25 shows an all-women troupe of dancers from Tuxtepec. This market town, the second-largest municipality in Oaxaca, is in the region called the Papaloapan, a lush lowland valley district in the northern part of the state. Just 20,944 of the 144,555 citizens counted in the 2005 census spoke an indigenous language. Fifty percent worked in agriculture, 13 percent in industry, and 33 percent in the service sector. The annual fiesta of this prosperous town has an elected queen, a parade of floats, and events with mounted cowboys. Tourism already flourishes there, but since there is little industry in the area, continued regular publicity through the Guelaguetza remains critical.

This troupe's contribution, the *flor de piña* (pineapple dance), is featured in every Guelaguetza, including the summary forms performed in hotels. The dancers' ceremonial dresses vary considerably in color and figuration but are nevertheless congruent in density of visual effect; each young woman carries a pineapple on her shoulder. The dance is always a crowd favorite, perhaps due to its focus on moves echoing a cancan or Rockettes maneuver. The dance is in three sections. An announcer delivers an opening speech (in Spanish only) as the dancers proceed onto and around the stage, turning to the right and left in smooth alternation to a melody in a quick 3/4 played by the state band (the group from Tlaxiaco used their own municipal wind band). During the extended middle section, lines of dancers form elegant shapes onstage, somewhat like marching bands at American football games. The dancers sometimes carry the pineapples and sometimes set them down. In one section, they dance around them. The last section of the performance echoes the first in music and footwork. This dance was elaborately choreographed for this stage in 1958 by a professor named Paulina Sofía Ocampo, who often still attends performances of the dance and is routinely acknowledged as its inventor. It's a powerful exaggeration of a traditional dance, a fifteen-minute display more vivid than varied.

Figure 26 shows the troupe from San Antonino, a small town not far from Oaxaca, near the wood-carving village of San Martín Tilcajete. Some 874 of the 4,829 citizens counted in 2005 speak Zapotec, and equal numbers engage in agriculture and the service sector. The town is known for its pretty church and for the famous wedding dresses made by many of its women. San Antonino's contribution to the Guelaguetza advertises this craft; the troupe performs a condensed depiction of a wedding. After the procession onto the stage, their "Fandango" starts with a double speech, the male in Zapotec, then the female in Spanish, praising and describing the traditions of the municipality. Then, as the state band plays a tune in 6/8, the playlet unfolds. The groom's family and friends are visiting those of the bride; they enter a receiving line before an altar (one with tables and a trussed turkey by its side) and are greeted couple by couple. The visitors sit in a pair of lines extending across the stage from the altar and are given ferns (as in figure 26) and little flasks of tequila. Then they dance in a half-dozen short sections contrasting in tempo and meter to fill out their fifteen minutes of exposure. The other weddings (*bodas*) and public celebrations of religious occasions (*mayordomías*) peppering the sequence of community contributions to the Guelaguetza contrast a bit in narrative ingredients, but all end in similar series of dances. While the approach of the group from Tlaxiaco was a medley within the medley that is the Guelaguetza's total composite staged performance, San Antonino's contribution is a fiesta within the entire fiesta, an example of "nested" folkloric intensification rather like that of the carved wooden pig painted with pigs discussed in the previous chapter. A few more playlets end with dances in recent Guelaguetzas than did previously. Another trend today is toward looking for new communities—often relatively small towns—to participate in and theoretically benefit from the event.

Figure 27 shows a troupe from Ixcatlán, a municipality of 9,625 in 2005, overwhelmingly Mazatec Indian and agricultural. Like Tuxtepec, Ixcatlán is in the Papaloapan, but "upstream," in a narrow valley now abutting a reservoir. Only 28 percent of the municipality has potable water, and the town is not on any well-traveled routes—this community is much less prosperous than those discussed earlier, and it would welcome tourism *starting*. The ensemble from Ixcatlán performs a medley of dances under the title "La Puta Chichi" (Chichi the Prostitute). The various sections include ones in which men mime asking women to dance, the resultant dance (a section like a two-step), a drunk section, one featuring kiss stealing, and so on. There are modern features (here, the obvious two-step shown in the photograph; compare this modern touch with Tlaxiaco's contribution, which features a twentieth-century song and a woman playing a wind instrument) and at least one obviously antiquated one, the string band in which two guitars are strummed and a harp plucked. This is one of the medley contributions, the majority genre, but through its unique features adds to the overall texture of the event, and is new to audiences who have witnessed the other three acts I have discussed at many, many Guelaguetzas.

| Table 3 | | |
|---|---|---|
| Homes of Dance Delegations at 1995 and 2002 Guelaguetzas; Aspects of Dances | | |
| 1995 | | |
| Delegation's Home | Women's Dance Outfits | Formations and Features |
| 1. Oaxaca City | "chinas" with head burdens | mostly a parade |
| 2. Huautla de Jiménez | red and blue skirt stripes | second section involves turkey |
| 3. San Melchior Betaza | white dresses with red sashes | line dances |
| 4. Juchitán de Zaragoza | silk/satin with embroidery | line dance; song "La Llorona" |
| 5. Santiago Juxtlahuaca | all men, in masks | bullfights; "girl" is matador |
| 6. Huahuapan de León | flowered skirt with ribbons | plus song "Canción Mixteca" |
| 7. San Miguel Sola de Vega | flowered skirt | line dances; song |
| 8. Pinotepa Nacional | single-color skirts; lace | inc. bullfight |
| 9. Tuxtepec | colorful; pineapples | usual pineapple dance |
| 10. Ejutla de Crespo | pastel skirts; black stripes | kissing dance |
| 11. Tlacolula de Matamoros | red skirts; rebozos; two big balloons | lots of hand kissing; mock wedding |
| 12. Zaachila | usual Pluma outfits | normal Danza de la Pluma |

## Shaping the Guelaguetza on the Hill

The organizers of the Guelaguetza hold to certain patterns in ordering the dances. In table 3, I illustrate these progressions in the list of troupes dancing the first Monday in 1995 and the second Monday in 2002. First there is an unvarying bold frame. The first ensemble to perform consists of women (only) from the city of Oaxaca. Each of these *chinas* (pretty young women) holds on her head a large basket containing a sculpture made of flowers. The women parade in, swaying their skirts to and fro, preceded by a few of the *gigantes* or *monos* that often participate in religious parades (the people inside these oversized human figures peek out at about the navel level). Balancing this at the end of the day (in events through 2003) is an all-male Danza de la Pluma ensemble. Here men wear large flowered headdresses and leap energetically as they express their Zapotec ancestors' happiness at Cortez's triumph over the Aztecs

| Table 3 (continued) | | |
| --- | --- | --- |
| Homes of Dance Delegations at 1995 and 2002 Guelaguetzas; Aspects of Dances | | |
| **2002** | | |
| Delegation's Home | Women's Dance Outfits | Formations and Features |
| 1. Oaxaca City* | "chinas" with head burdens | mostly a parade |
| 2. Huautla de Jiménez* | red and blue skirt stripes | line dances; inc. song |
| 3. San Melchior Betaza | white dresses with red sashes | line dances |
| 4. San Pablo Macuiltianguis | bordado dresses | very tangled bullfights |
| 5. Tlacolula de Matamoros | | parade/dance mayordomía |
| 6. Ciudad Ixtepec | very fancy dresses | inc. hit song "Zandunga" |
| 7. Juchitán de Zaragoza | inc. elaborate head pieces | girls feign sleep; waltz |
| 8. Santiago Juxtlahuaca | all men, in masks | bullfights, with horns! |
| 9. Tlaxiaco | black skirts; bordado tops | line dance; men are bulls |
| 10. Ejutla de Crespo* | pastel skirts; black stripes | partly sung; kiss stealing |
| 11. Putla de Guerrero | skirts with lots of lace | sectional; women are bulls |
| 12. Santa Catarina Juquila | satin; bordado tops | mayordomía and sexy quips |
| 13. San Juan Bautista Tuxtepec* | all women; pineapple dance dresses | usual fancy pineapple dance |
| 14. Culiapan de Guerrero | unsurprising Pluma outfits | Danza de la Pluma again |
| *These delegations danced both Mondays during the year in question. | | |

(initially considered a positive development by the Aztecs' vassals). The story can be involved—and closer to understandable as historical narrative—back in the villages, where the dance takes hours, but it is reduced to one long series of leaps here. The audience understands some of what the dance is about because the story has been told and retold and because these dance outfits are the only ones in the event that appear pre-Hispanic (see figures 3 and 28).

Next in reliability of placement to those framing ensembles is the pineapple dance I discussed earlier, which comes near the end (ninth of twelve ensembles in the 1995 event, thirteenth of fourteen in 2002). Other patterns of placing ensembles in the sequence of performance also hold over the decades. The most general rule is that simpler medleys of dances alternate with ones featuring any flashy novelty. Specific

Figure 28. Dances excerpted from village tradition for the Guelaguetza continue to be employed in their much-longer historic forms in festivals at home. Here the Danza de la Pluma, traditional in many villages in Oaxaca's Valles Centrales, is performed in Teotitlán del Valle for the Fiesta Titular en Honor a la Preciosa Sangre de Cristo (June 27–July 12, 1999). The dance outfits vary from town to town in the central valleys. The pictorial woven panels on the dancers' backs honor the rug-making mercantile focus of Teotitlán.

ensembles turn up in customary positions in the roster each time they participate, so that the regular attendee will witness a welcome mix of the familiar with a few surprises each year. For instance, the ensemble from Huautla de Jiménez (from a mountainous area in northwest Oaxaca state) performs fairly straightforward line dances punctuated by verses of song. The women's dresses are white with embroidered flowers and clusters of lateral light blue and carmine ribbon stripes (see the third woman in the Diosa Centeotl pageant shown in figure 29). I have heard that their dance includes a reference to a priest's experience with the hallucinogenic mushrooms characteristic of their part of the mountains and, more generally, that fertilization of flowers also makes an appearance, but this information remains in an oral tradition known to few members of the audience. To most in attendance, this performance is simply an attractive array of line dances ornamented with a usual complement of humorous flirting. Nothing in these fragments of dance tells us why it belongs in the second spot on most Monday's rosters—the accompanying song, which might be illuminating, is in the local indigenous language, Mazateco—but this dance retains its position in the sequence year after year.

Like the crafts discussed in the previous chapter, folkloric performances lose some meaning when moved from detailed cultural contexts to displays intended for new, unevenly informed audiences. But just as with crafts, such loss can be balanced through the same three kinds of intensification. The most common type, intensification through addition, takes place when Indians wearing many different outfits perform a series of contrasting dances within short amounts of time, each act adding to the overall density and amount of information. Second, intensification through selection occurs when striking items are drawn from tradition, even if those items are thin in terms of amount of information. The dances from Huautla de Jiménez furnish an example; in fact, those dances have lost information in recent times. Until the late 1990s, three or four dancers carried products characteristic of the area, including a turkey. No one I asked knew why the turkey no longer appears, though I gathered that it had been present simply to show that turkeys were important in the local economy, rather than as part of local myth or religion, and perhaps were dispensable for that reason. In any case, removing the turkey resulted in a visually less crowded performance, one with a tighter focus on the gorgeous huipiles, providing good contrast with the visually busier flanking acts. There are still a few turkeys not enjoying their last days on earth in other dances at every Guelaguetza; turkeys are important fiesta ingredients throughout rural Oaxaca. Third, we witness throughout the event intensification through virtuosity: the expert precision of dancers' moves strengthens the overall impact.

**Table 4**

**How the Guelaguetza Includes All the Normal Ingredients of Mexican Fiestas**

| FIESTA INGREDIENT | MANIFESTATION AT THE GUELAGUETZA | LOCATION |
|---|---|---|
| Popular dances | 1. Guelaguetza on the hill<br>2. Evening presentations by individual delegations<br>3. Other presentations by clubs, by children, in hotels, etc. | 1. Hill auditorium<br>2. Santo Domingo<br>3. Places N of square |
| Music | For the above dancing; state marimbas and other year-round performances; at ancillary events; in all parades; by mariachis and others on square (concerts early, for diners later); beggars | At above locations; on square; in markets; on all main streets |
| Religious ceremonies | At Carmen Alto and at a smaller church (thus calendric fiestas partially absorbed into this larger fortnight-long festival) | NW of square 4 and 6 blocks respectively |
| Processionals | For above ceremonies; by chirimías early on the mornings of the Guelaguetza and by dance delegations evenings before | Above locations; on streets north of square |
| Electing a queen | Diosa Centeotl chosen from among representatives of individual delegations the day before the first Guelaguetza | 4 blocks N of square at Santo Domingo Church |
| Carnival rides and games | 1. Rides: Ferris wheel plus other rotating mechanical rides<br>2. Games: balls-into-holes, etc., all easy, with small prizes<br>3. Tiro al blanco: shooting targets to win old-style songs | 1. 8 blocks NNE<br>2. Within markets<br>3. Within markets |
| Sport contests | 1. Basic variety sports<br>2. Half-marathon and bicycle race | 1. At university<br>2. Finish downtown |
| Food | 1. Usual regional snacks in unusual quantities<br>2. Regional Festival of Sweets<br>3. Regional Festival of Mescal | 1. Market; stairs to hill;<br>2. Shopping streets N<br>3. 8 blocks N of square |
| Markets and other sales | 1. Local crafts: rugs, carvings, black pottery, etc.<br>2. Crafts from elsewhere in Mexico<br>3. Anything poor people would customarily buy at markets | 1. Crowded square<br>2. Park 8 blocks north<br>3. Crowded square |
| Other (here: pageants) | 1. Bani Stui Gulal (repetition from antiquity), supposedly the history of the Guelaguetza; college kids showing skin<br>2. Legend of the Princess Donaji (Romeo and Juliet? Aida?) | 1. Formerly near Soledad; auditorium<br>2. Auditorium |

## The Guelaguetza as a Traditional Festival

Toward the end of the show, we are ready to welcome the familiar Danza de la Pluma, performed by one or another ensemble from the central valleys. We soon leave, overloaded by the barrage of impressions. This might seem like a good time to rest, but many visitors prefer to continue to celebrate. Indeed, to make the Guelaguetza sufficiently attractive to all involved requires experiencing more than the event itself, which is confined to a mere three hours or so on two occasions separated by a week.[4] Tourists invest substantial time and money to get to Oaxaca and anticipate days rather than just hours of entertainment. Also, over half of these tourists are Mexican and therefore share a model of how a festival ought to be shaped both with the occupants of the free seats and with the performers. That model is the paradigmatic Mexican fiesta based on each town's observances of its patron saint's day, an annual event that typically constitutes a very full weekend. So activities related to or supplementing the staged dances have gradually accumulated to flank the Mondays on the hill. Table 4 shows how the weeks of the Guelaguetza manage to encompass most of the usual fiesta ingredients. Yes, dance is much more central than at a typical village fiesta, but other customary ingredients have burgeoned on the coattails of the Guelaguetza's core element of dance. In short, a display designed as a pair of discrete events extracted from village festivals by the state tourist board and intellectuals has thus become an enormous, diverse, but in many ways truly traditional festival.

Most village festivals begin at the church: these holidays center on the local holy days. Much of the Guelaguetza publicity—tourist brochures, newspaper articles, and now Web sites—asserts that this factor lies behind the choice of dates for the Guelaguetza, too. The fiesta for the Virgin at the church of Carmen Alto (a half-dozen blocks north of the square) supposedly spawned the modern Guelaguetza. But today this church-centered fiesta simply introduces a busier fortnight (though not busier for parishioners of the neighborhood church, who are intensely involved in their own festival). People in town for the larger fiesta will notice its prelude in passing, but their "church" part of the Guelaguetza consists of touring the big cathedrals and perhaps staying once or twice for mass. The fiesta of Carmen Alto centers on activities inside the church, that is, special masses and clusters of baptisms, first communions, and confirmations all scheduled to be part of the special occasion. In addition, there is a processional headed by men carrying the church's banners, accompanied by a brass band made up of members of the church, a band that plays later in front of the church. A half-dozen women staffing snack stands in front of the church raise funds efficiently. Last, in many a church courtyard, men affix fireworks to lath scaffolds. Lighting the type of scaffold that is generally the largest, a tower several stories high, caps an evening display. Most of the others are set off during a parade to the front of the church. The man bearing the most popular item, a handheld schematic bull, charges toward the audience while little firecrackers launch from the lath frame toward the feet of his randomly chosen prey.

Mexican religious festivals always include processions like the one described, and so must the Guelaguetza, though the principle of the procession ends up parceled out into several different gestures. Before dawn on the two Mondays of the Guelaguetza, the chirimías of several villages assemble outside the cathedral on the square and start parading (while playing) toward the hill auditorium at about 6:00. The word *chirimía* has an immediate and a general meaning. It is a specific musical instrument, a crude double reed best classified as a shawm, probably descended from sixteenth-century Spanish versions (as are many Latin American plucked stringed instruments). More broadly, a village chirimía is a pipe-and-drum ensemble of a type formerly employed to accompany religious processions, a function now normally assumed by the village brass band.

The few surviving village chirimías (ensembles) of Oaxaca each include a handful of drums (often cast-off old snare drums from brass bands) and one or two loud wind instruments (bugles, whistles, or rarely an actual double-reed chirimía). While the specific instrument types in Oaxaca's few remaining local chirimías trace their roots to Europe, the general idea of pipe-and-drum ensembles that accompany processionals is an ancient one in both old and new worlds. But these chirimías, having largely given up that function, have the climax of their year in the fore-concert to the Guelaguetza. Old men and young boys, playing out of tune and in dubious rhythm, perform stock medleys often beginning with "Mañanitas" (the Mexican birthday song) and ending with the final phrases of the "Jarabe Tapatio" (Mexican Hat Dance).

Other links between the Guelaguetza and the processional as a fiesta component include those already briefly mentioned, that is, the short processionals connected with church fiestas during the Guelaguetza fortnight, the slow march onto the stage of the Diosa Centeotl (corn goddess) before the dances, a five-minute processional with which the Chinas Oaxaqueñas precede their dance (led in by the combined chirimías, functional at last), and the formal entries of each dance ensemble. But the main processionals take place on Sunday evenings, when dance troupes pass through the city streets of the old town, sometimes marching and sometimes dancing. Several troupes will march together, preceded by a few gigantes. The streets are so crowded that one can barely see the dancers, but the event nevertheless functions as an enjoyable advertisement of the mornings on the hill.

A few other fiesta ingredients have modest but real presences during the Guelaguetza fortnight. Oaxaca's state university sponsors tournaments in track and field, swimming, volleyball, baseball, karate, soccer, tennis, and chess. These aren't seen by most tourists, but a half-marathon includes stretches through the city streets, as does a bicycle race made dangerous by downtown's close quarters and some cobblestone streets. Rural fiestas often include a rodeo, but as far as I could tell, the rodeo was the single common fiesta ingredient absent from the Guelaguetza fortnight. Carnival rides are restricted to a handful of rusty Ferris wheels and the like that generally set up next to the northerly Juarez Park. Games appear within the complex of market stands. Many are simple and easy-to-win ball-in-holes games aimed at children: the prizes are cheaper than the tickets, but the kids have fun. All these standard games and rides are owned and operated by families that tour the state, going from one festival to another in an annual cycle.

Tourists may dine at restaurants that specialize in Oaxaca regional fare all year: all food contrasting with what they consume back home is carnival food to them. Food stands in the extended market feature *tlayudas*, a regional large tortilla—this is the fiesta food for the poor. And there are ancillary festivals of sweets (local *dulces* are distinctive and tempting), cheese (pale, highly textured *quesillo* dominates), and local mescal. This subsidiary festival is the largest affair nested within the Guelaguetza, and one must actually pay admission to an extended display and sampling lineup north at the Juarez Park. Markets in general are bigger than usual during these weeks, too. All manner of stands appear incrementally, situated farther and farther into the square and down contiguous streets as the Guelaguetza approaches until downtown is stunningly crowded. Much of what is offered represents normal market fare, ranging from pirated CDs to cheap kitchenware, thus illustrating a simple proportional response to the temporary swelling of the population of the city during this festival season. But there are also special genre-specific markets that target tourists or the festivity-loosened purse strings of the local upper class. One such seasonal market features Oaxaca crafts (on the square); another has crafts from elsewhere in Mexico (at the Juarez Park; the entrepreneurs are from Oaxaca).

Two supposedly historical pageants are intended to help us understand the cultural backdrop for the Guelaguetza. The Bani Stui Gulal (repetition from antiquity) offers four tableaux that symbolize points in the history of Mexico and include dances. This takes place each Sunday of the extended festival. The evening after each Guelaguetza features the Legend of Princess Donaji, Donaji being the name of a Zapotec Juliet (or Aida?) who fell in love with a Mixtec Romeo (Radames?) of long ago. There's love, disaster, and sacrifice, with the flavor of a mid-nineteenth-century Italian opera. The pageant is historically dubious and dramatically overdrawn, but it attracts thousands.

But the greatest pageant takes place on a pair of mornings shortly before the first Guelaguetza. Since the festival theoretically descends from precontact rites for a corn goddess, a human embodiment called the Diosa Centeotl is chosen each year from among contestants drawn from the visiting dance troupes, one aspirant per troupe. This competition, though run like a one-day beauty pageant (extended over two days more recently), focuses less on physical attributes than on speeches in which the contestants efficiently and humorously present "authentic" knowledge of their home's traditions (especially of the elaborate local folk clothing they wear) and glorious history, usually narrated first in an indigenous tongue, then in Spanish. Many contestants incorporate

Figure 29. Each year, in a pageant that precedes the Guelaguetza, representatives of all the delegations that will dance that year compete for the title of Diosa Centeotl (corn goddess). The girl who gives the most thorough, spunky speech about her village's traditions wins. The winners in 2007 were, from left to right, the new Diosa Centeotl, from Juchitán de Zaragoza; the second-place winner, from Ejutla de Crespo; and the third-place winner, from Huautla de Jiménez.

gender-based humor into their shouted speeches, and the one with the best combination of spunk and knowledge of tradition wins. The first- through third-place winners from 2007 are pictured in figure 29. The winner, from Juchitán, was teary-eyed, following the Miss America model; the second-place winner, from Ejutla de Crespo, presented a stoic look; and the woman who took third, from Huautla de Jiménez, retained the aggressive spirit that made her my favorite in the competition—she clearly resented not winning!

I have saved music for last in this review of how standard fiesta ingredients make their presence known in the Guelaguetza, but this ingredient is indispensable and part of every dance performance. A fairly standard repertory of tunes is employed for extra Guelaguetzas on the city square, often by young dancers-in-training who sat on their parents' laps on the bus to Oaxaca. In addition, an old folks' club puts on their idiosyncratic version of the Guelaguetza twice, and several hotels put on *their* versions as many times as is commercially viable (the same hotels

that offer a mini-Guelaguetza with dinner a few times a week throughout the year). When you add all of this to the regular Oaxaca city musical fare—weekly evenings from the state marimba, Sunday concerts by
the state brass band, evening strolling mariachi bands (and one norteña
band, and more marimbas)—the music and dance calendar for late July
is packed. Also, aside from the calendar of discrete events, there is the
music of the *tiro al blanco* carnival game, in which successful marksmen
win songs seemingly performed by marionettes (see figure 38 and the
accompanying discussion in the next chapter). Last, visitors hear music
played by dozens of beggars who descend on the city for this fortnight,
men who play selections from the same narrow range of older musical
genres as the tiro al blanco game stocks, the rhythms of which we hear
at the Guelaguetza.

Thus the Guelaguetza is far more than three hours of display scheduled on two successive Mondays. It is echoed in shortened performances and supplemented by the usual fiesta components, so that the two
weeks of individual events coalesce into a giant unity serving tourists
and all populations of locals simultaneously. But the composite fiesta
would not be possible without its core, the volunteer efforts of the dancers and musicians who travel from all over the state. Who are they, and
what does the Guelaguetza mean to them? How are they chosen? How
are the dances they bring from their homes shaped (or reshaped) to fit
on the Guelaguetza stage?

### Participants in the Guelaguetza

Various villages have clubs that cultivate older dances for their own use
at their own festivals and also potentially for the Guelaguetza. Many
members are single young people who belong to relatively high-status
families. These youngsters' families can afford for them to take time to
learn dances in a social situation, and can afford the price—in money,
but perhaps even more so in time—to make or otherwise obtain a suitable dance outfit. Why do these youths want to dance? For some it is
a social activity, pure and simple. Many participants told me they just
wanted the chance to go to the big city and have fun (cf. Titon 1999).
Their banter and sidelong glances at one another made clear that a

critical ingredient in that fun is flirting. For others, a factor more old-fashioned enters the picture, the *promesa* (a serious vow addressed to the supernatural). One common theme is health: a dancer can ask for a return of someone to good health or give thanks for that having taken place (José de los Angeles, the Teotitlán weaver who made the rug pictured in figure 17, made the promesa when he was in his early twenties; also see Gagnier de Mendoza 2005, 125). But the other most common promesa theme among dancers I interviewed was to offer up the effort of the dance for the opportunity to find a good partner in life. That is, dancing for (the) god(s) banks a storehouse of virtue that might eventually be rewarded by the happy circumstance of meeting the right person for marriage. Of course, there is no clean line between a promesa intended to facilitate courting and the fact that being in the dance club places a young person in the company of suitable future mates. Romance and social cohesion are served in both processes. How participants are chosen similarly mixes the modern and the traditional. In some towns, the mayor simply picks the dancers. In contrast, in Teotitlán del Valle, a man who wishes to portray Montezuma in the Danza de la Pluma must furnish a three-pig feast to the town.

The shaping of each Guelaguetza on the hill begins when an "authenticity committee" of anthropologists and other upper-class culture mavens visits sizable native towns. The committee views dances presented by hopeful local culture organizations, and assesses authenticity (and, more quietly, aesthetics and logistics, that is, both the intrinsic attractiveness of an act to an outsider audience and how that sequence might fit with others during a given year). Judging tradition might seem academically or philosophically tricky, but it's simple enough as done here. Checking authenticity just means making sure that there is no plastic in the outfits, no rock dancing, nothing that will seem jarringly modern to audiences. The amount of traditional features is not regulated—that is, if one embroidered flower on a woman's shoulder is traditional, a dozen of the same will be equally acceptable. Folkloric intensification of each of the kinds outlined earlier is rampant, indeed encouraged, so that all presentations at the Guelaguetza will be vivid and reasonably congruent not just in length but in generous ration of visual and musical information. The authenticity committee has in the past suggested refinements in choreography to suit the orientation of the stage and the fact that many viewers will be sitting far away. Dancers will retain the traditional steps but also assemble in lines, circles, or other formations that can give a macro-shape to the dance. The dances are ordered to maximize contrast between successive groups and also to frame the series with the two ensembles most visually dramatic because of their use of massive headdresses, as explained earlier.

The drastic shortening of village performances for the Guelaguetza is balanced by recommended adjustments, since these tend toward intensification of effect through increased decoration and choices of especially telling moments in the home dances. Neither process seems to bother the performers much, and perhaps the truncation and intensification balance out for them, too. I asked some dancers from Teotitlán del Valle how they felt about their seven-hour Danza de la Pluma being reduced to ten minutes (I give a picture of a moment from their own form of the dance in figure 28). Was it robbed of its meaning? "That's just a show we put on for the state and the tourists; we know what it really means, and *some* in the audience know too," I was told repeatedly (on longer forms of these dances, see Harris 2000; Dallal 1997; and Peterson 1968). In contrast, the village of Zaachila, which also presents the Danza de la Pluma at the Guelaguetza, does not have a long version at home. They acquired (or reacquired) this dance tradition after the Guelaguetza was in place, and learned a digest of it as their essential form.

The contrast between compressed rituals and dances adopted from the Guelaguetza is apparent to outsiders only through evening performances between the Mondays when individual delegations offer two-hour presentations of their own in separate concerts. Some delegations present richer and more coherent versions of their region's danced folklore; other groups have the Guelaguetza as their source for dance tradition, and therefore know dances from towns other than their own, and present a mini-Guelaguetza as their evening performance. Both approaches seem to work fine for dancers and audiences. The individuals most likely to be troubled by the wild variations in processes nurturing tradition are in fact the intellectuals who are likely to be on the committee for authenticity. "But this is for the state and the economy: we don't let it get too crazy, but we bend quite a bit," explained Margarita

Figure 30. The winner of the main division of the 1999 Night of the Radishes, a remarkable contest and display (on Oaxaca's main square, shortly before Christmas) of carvings from radishes (not the petite North American radishes: these grow to resemble enormous red carrots). This carving portrayed the Guelaguetza, reproducing costumes in remarkable detail: two Tehuana women are in front, with a man outfitted for the Danza de la Pluma between and slightly behind them. On the Night of the Radishes, see Méndez Aquino 1990.

Figure 31. The Super Mercado Guelaguetza, a five-and-dime general store in downtown Oaxaca named for the festival, as are a hotel, a brand of chocolate, sweets stands, et cetera.

Dalton Palomo, a prominent anthropologist and frequent member of the authenticity committee. She went on to tell me that a coastal dance celebration clings to the letter of tradition more faithfully, and that scholars and other intellectuals let the greater authenticity and lesser commercialism of that event balance their personal qualms about the Guelaguetza.

The impact of these endorsed, reshaped, and prominently publicly performed dances is incredible. Granted, there is no shortage of romantic excess in both rhetoric and interpretation. Traditions said to hearken back to preconquest or early colonial times contain plenty of ingredients in apparel, movement, and especially sound that reach back no further than the nineteenth century. The actual youth and the barely acknowledged indigenous-Spanish hybridity of most dances—that they really have changed plenty and recently, contrary to rhetoric asserting stasis—may explain the ease with which adjustments made specifically for the Guelaguetza can be accepted back home. The citizens of Zaachila are as happy with their Guelaguetza-shaped pan-Oaxacan tradition as are the citizens of Teotitlán del Valle with their older and more detailed Danza de la Pluma.

By now, the Guelaguetza's short dances and accompanying tunes constitute a canon worthy of emulation and exploitation. It is not just that the most famous dances are performed by small ensembles in three hotels in Oaxaca City throughout the year and may be taken on tour throughout Mexico and abroad to advertise the allure of Oaxaca. The Guelaguetza has become the signature event of Oaxaca. All kinds of things in Oaxaca are named Guelaguetza: a hotel, a small general store (see figure 31), a bakery, a brand of chocolate. Representations of dancers are sold as dolls and tin Christmas ornaments and in books and videos of each Guelaguetza. The event may be crude in term of authenticity (by any definition), and it certainly includes many ingredients younger than claimed. But it remains crucial to the economy and politics of the state of Oaxaca, is enjoyed by most residents of the state, and is enormously popular with tourists of differing backgrounds.

## What Does—or Should—the Guelaguetza Mean?

In the end, what kinds of pictures of the state of Oaxaca does the Guelaguetza offer, and to whom? Tourists who journey to Oaxaca may concentrate on one side of tourism, "switching off" while relaxing in cafés on the square (Krippendorf 1987, 23). As they move lazily toward the mode of ethnic tourism, they can be satisfied with "surgically detached" "ethnographic fragments" (Kirshenblatt-Gimblett 1998a, 14). But other tourists have come on a romantic quest to view an embodiment of an earlier, presumably better—and to them certainly more exotic—way of life; "holiday" closer to its ancestral meaning of "holy day" (Graburn 1989, 26). For these "ethnic tourists" (following Van Den Berghe), the Guelaguetza offers a marvelously flexible experience, an efficient visual trip around indigenous Oaxaca for visitors who have little time, and an introduction to a more thorough visit for those staying longer. After tourists briefly view the gorgeous huipiles worn by women from Huautla de Jiménez, they can return between the Mondays of the Guelaguetza to the city's museums, read about the meanings woven into that garb, and thus contextualize and enrich their memories of the scant but grueling hours of pleasure on the hill.

The state government draws on the event as much for political purposes as for economic ones. One hears repeatedly that the visiting delegations represent "the seven regions" of the state, a characterization that stipulates diversity even as it asserts that the seven regions constitute a viable whole (the mantra like list of regions: "¡Papaloapan, Sierra, Valles Centrales, Cañada, Costa, Istmo, Mixteca!"). The Guelaguetza brings native, local mestizo, and national and international tourist populations together in a way that implicitly declares that the indigenous populations are happy, healthy, and exotic in a benign way: they decorate the state. The tight control that visiting dance troupes endure during the Guelaguetza suggests that the populations they represent, populations that we are intended to accept as standing for all of indigenous Oaxaca, could not possibly be unruly or in any way unhappy.

However, all who travel to Oaxaca witness evidence of poverty and turmoil. Any visit entails spending time on Oaxaca's large and charming main square. Shops, plush hotels, and especially high-end restaurants surround most of the square, but the south side fronts on the government palace. As mentioned in my preface, the long eaves of this large building often provide shelter for one or another protest encampment. In 2002 a new group arrived from rural Las Huertas, Teojomulco. They followed a customary pattern—they set out bedding, built campfires, posted numerous hand-lettered protest signs, and began begging for financial support from passersby, many of whom are tourists. In addition, during that year's Guelaguetza, the protest leaders, acting in concert with a variety of small antigovernment political groups, directly addressed the discrepancy between their plight and the happy prosperity of rural life as portrayed in the fiesta. The night before the first Monday, when the dance delegations paraded through the streets of the old city, the protesters paraded too and in other small but visible ways made their unhappiness public. The point made to tourists was that not all of rural Oaxaca is in good shape. And while reasonably heedless teenagers make up most of the Guelaguetza's dance troupes, not all dancers are willing to be complicit in their being caricatured as happy people possessing charming folklore. During the years that families from the government-ravaged village of San Agustín Loxicha lived on the square (1997–2002), dance delegations (particularly central valley groups presenting the Danza de la Pluma) would occasionally put on a show on their behalf, performing in the street bordering the protest encampment while surrounded by protest banners (see figure 3).

The Guelaguetza purports to build bridges between socioeconomic classes in Oaxaca, and also between Mexican and foreign tourists, between tourists and locals via different but compatible feelings of nostalgia, between indigenous peoples and their own complex pasts, and so on. It will doubtless continue being staged into the foreseeable future, not just for compelling economic reasons but because it means so many things to so many people. But what about those Indians represented by the women and children residing on Oaxaca's main square? Does the relative prosperity of the natives who dance just rub salt in the protesters' wounds? I close the chapter with another visit to the Diosa Centeotl pageant. The winner in 2001 was a Triqui, a member of the small and beleaguered population, members of which were the principal protest marchers a decade ago. Quite a few Triqui still can be seen every day on the square, but as lowest-rung ambulatory merchants serving tourists. They sell gardenias, swiftly woven headbands and wristlets, crudely carved wooden letter openers, and so on. The lives of these particular Triqui cannot be described as prosperous, but they have moved up several steps from their worst times (see Amnesty International 1986, 1990; and also Mata Garcia 1986).

Having a Triqui become the Diosa Centeotl asserted a connection between poor and not-so-poor Indians. Newspaper coverage of the young woman, Concepción Martínez Merino, cited her ethnic derivation more often than in other years. Her election as corn goddess offered yet another temporally compact but symbolically rich event. Like every moment at the Guelaguetza, the event succeeded because it conveyed different acceptable messages to the various populations witnessing it. A uniting theme was that problems in the countryside could be resolved. Conflicting messages branched out to the different populations at the Guelaguetza. The ruling elite could believe this moment symbolized their benevolence and their continuing skill in managing affairs of state. They were keeping Oaxaca stable, a viable political entity, a place safe for themselves and for the economically critical populace of tourists.

Those tourists could imagine that unhappiness in Oaxaca would not nurture a rebel force parallel to the Zapatistas in Chiapas, and that populations whose plight gained publicity through their delegations' residence on the square could melt back into the general indigenous population in time. It was not simply that these tourists could set aside pinpricks of worry about personal safety but also that they could mentally return these indigenous groups from an uncomfortable present to the romantic world of the Guelaguetza, a world of aesthetic vibrancy coupled with lively embodiments of nostalgia. And what of the indigenous people and the lower class in general? Having a Triqui sitting by the governor's side in public, however briefly, offered an olive branch to the poor, even those poor whose frustration periodically boiled over into violence, imprisonment, and protest—a message intended to offer real hope.

# 4.

# Southern Mexican Contemporary Traditional Culture That Is Little Affected by Tourism

What can we learn about living tradition from the apron a woman wears as she sells produce in a southern Mexican market, from the shopping basket in which a customer carries some of that produce away, from the words adorning the truck that brought the saleswoman and her family's crops to town, and even from the music playing on that truck's radio? These illustrate down-home, often regional practices learned from person to person. They mark processes of creation and consumption that reinforce layered identities that exemplify thriving contemporary traditional culture. Of special significance, these traditional items and practices are shaped and used in ways largely unaffected by tourism, ways that would survive the departure of that economically critical, culture-transforming industry.

Thriving untouched by tourism—or nearly so—really does make these genres noteworthy, since in southern Mexico, as in more than a few places in the third world, many genres of *inherited* traditional material culture and of traditional festive practices have been "preserved" through the infusion of tourist dollars. Moreover, as a paradoxical but unavoidable part of that process, the tourist-supported crafts and practices are profoundly transformed. They have experienced ruptures in tradition, ruptures inseparable from their having achieved acceptability as romanticized symbols among outsiders. They seldom serve historical practical functions any longer and, in insiders' collective psychology, constitute only somewhat reassuring *symbols of past symbols* of local identity—for example, a small, polished but porous black jug from San Bartolo Coyotepec partakes in local tradition by evoking memories of the large, functional gray jugs formerly made in that town and used in daily life there.

What does it mean when certain traditional genres dodge the shadow of tourism? Does the skewing of some branches of tradition—the parts "preserved" by romantic ethnic tourism—change the rest of the tree? What I discuss in this chapter represents a stream parallel to, and barely interacting with, the more visible river of tourist-supported tradition, although still reflecting participation in the modernizing world. Unsurprisingly, any classes of objects and practices employed in daily life will experience change—change resulting from the operation of aesthetic principles through unruly history, and also change reflecting negotiation between socioeconomically contrasting communities. Southern Mexico can stand for much of the third world in the potency and constant exercise of interlocking ferments that shape life both outside and within the world of tourism, tensions (1) between the few rich and many poor and whatever small population functions as a middle class, (2) in the complex cauldron of secular and sacred, and (3) pitting visions of culture that emphasize history and locale versus ones celebrating progress and internationality.

### The Public Markets: Choosing What to Study by Discovering Where to Work

My interest in aprons, baskets, and sayings painted on vehicles coalesced gradually, initially as a by-product of longer-term research on tradition as a factor in the shaping and consumption of commercial pop music. I made repeated visits to Oaxaca beginning in the late 1980s to study musical life. My daily routine fell into different compartments. I worked steadily, but not all day, every day. My family and I bought souvenirs during hours that were relatively informal in intellectual terms, hours spent seeking the casually serendipitous intersections between personal aesthetics and the sincere—if seldom analytically rigorous—attention to authenticity characteristic of ethnic tourism. It was precisely when my interest in the signature crafts of the area became more self-consciously academic that I began to wonder if I would also be able to pin down a "control group" of products or behaviors that issued from traditional life but were not transformed by tourism, despite flourishing alongside those intercultural profit engines. An important question arose immediately: where should I look? My research on tradition in musical life had led me to the largest public markets and to the streets that working people traversed to get to those markets. In contrast, the souvenirs that my family and I bought were generally displayed in prettier, cleaner parts of town, locations where tourists tended to reside and circulate. The geographic division was not clean; tourists occasionally sampled local color by visiting the markets. However, in those markets, souvenirs representing the older traditional crafts for which Oaxaca is justly famous occupied a segregated few rows of stands, thus colonizing clearly defined corners within a larger space that continued to belong primarily to locals. That is, in those markets, the display and sale of objects with long-term traditional pedigrees—which are attractive to tourists—were largely physically separate from any contemporary traditional products and processes that working Mexicans could afford.

Historically, many regions initially defined by geography have also become and remain culturally unified regions in large part because citizens of given towns regularly attend easily accessible neighboring towns' markets both as sellers and as customers. These markets take us back to basics. Although one can buy a wide range of things somewhere in each, the collective economic and cultural anchor remains the sale of foodstuffs, with designated areas emphasizing in turn produce, meat, and, in coastal areas, seafood. Every market also features prepared food dispensed either from small taco stands with several kinds of meat sizzling on a single round grill or at full food stalls consisting of compact but versatile kitchens and long tables for diners.

The traditional material culture discussed in this chapter is clearly visible within or around the largest public markets in three large cities of southern Mexico: Oaxaca, San Cristóbal, and Mérida (capital of the state of Yucatán and the mercantile center for the entire Yucatán Peninsula). These three cities are the most important tourist centers for their respective states but are also metropolises with considerable economic vigor not linked to tourism. All three also follow a common demographic pattern in Latin America: big cities, run and largely populated by mestizos, are surrounded by Indian municipalities (Oaxaca is situated in Zapotec turf, the other two within Maya territory; Mérida is much more prosperous than the other two cities, and that distinction played a role in what I found there). I supplemented systematic visits to the markets in these big, tourist-infested cities with shorter trips to sizable towns in the orbit of the larger cities. Each of the central public markets I visited covers several square blocks plus several hundred meters on each street leading to those blocks; from the air, each market complex looks like a geometric caricature of a spider's body and segmented legs.

What characteristics would we expect to mark culture that is traditional but not tourist oriented? We can begin a definition through exclusions: we would expect that such classes of objects and practices would not be sold to or carried away in significant amounts by tourists, and would not partake in the basic processes that one can witness in the tourist-oriented crafts and festivities. The tourist-responsive processes result from souvenirs' collective divorce from inherited cultural roles (for example, adding sizes too little or too big to fulfill function) and a consequent heightened focus on symbol (detailed and solemn discussion of history and authenticity as part of the sales process) and on aesthetics (finding common ground between inherited typical appearances and shoppers' tastes, coupled with intensification of appearance by adding more colors, more decorations, etc.). And how did I decide that certain immune-to-tourism genres were nevertheless traditional? I followed a straightforward consensus definition of folkloric culture, seeking classes of things and behavior conjoining individual creativity with continuity (emphasizing continuity), embodying small-group artistic communication, and helping mark and advertise group identity.

Once I established that a substantial body of traditional public culture flourished outside the matrix of tourism and tradition, the nuances of how this worked became my focus: How clearly are contemporary traditional objects and processes of creation and use set apart from those of mass culture? How does variation work aesthetically? How

does the nature of and variation within genres help define folk populations? How does tradition still operate in touristed areas, tradition that
remains outside tourism and could survive the departure of tourism?

### Aprons Worn in the Markets

One historical focus of traditional material culture has been clothing.
However, in Oaxaca, though traditional homemade blouses and dresses
can be seen at formal folkloric events (e.g., the Guelaguetza) and ornament certain rites of passage (e.g., weddings among some conservative
affluent people), manufactured clothing dominates daily life, including the markets. However, handmade aprons are also worn in public
primarily in these same public markets. Several segments of the sales
force there wear aprons for somewhat different reasons. Some of the
younger women who sell garments or knickknacks sport aprons in solid
colors inscribed with the names of the small companies for which they
work. Many men and women who cut and sell meat or seafood protect their clothes with aprons in solid colors (often dark), often made of
slick, waterproof materials (this is the only situation in which many men
wear aprons). But a majority of aprons seen at the market are worn by
middle-aged or older women selling produce or meals, whether at full-
fledged market stands or simply sitting in an aisle next to a modest stack
of whatever crop their family produces.

In the state of Oaxaca, most market women's aprons look like those
worn by Isabel Gutierrez in figures 32 and 19. She is the Zapotec woman
we first met in chapter 2 selling her family's handmade rugs in a downtown market in Teotitlán del Valle. Oaxacan aprons are made of cotton
plaid or checked material; the extremely wide variety of small prints employed are all fairly subdued, offering visual textures rather than distinctive patterns. These aprons are slipped on over the head, then perhaps
tied and perhaps also buttoned in back. A few specialists make most of
these aprons, from the initial cutting to the final touches. This decorating, perhaps hand stitched but more often machine embroidered,
consists of flowers and leaves and associated swirls placed on the pair
of front pockets and sometimes the bodice, as well as, in many cases,
lace outlining the pockets, bodice, or both. The dresses protected by

Figure 32. Isabel Gutierrez in her market stall, July 2007. After a year of extremely poor sales (caused by the 2006 strikes and riots in downtown Oaxaca), her family's offerings included fewer expensive rugs, a direct Navajo copy (hanging behind her head), and more cut-rate napkins and tablecloths. Another symptom of hard times is the apron she is wearing, a Oaxaca-style garment identical in style and quality to those of poor women selling vegetables in Teotitlán's small produce market; compare this with the classier apron she wore in 1999 (figure 19).

these aprons are generally commercial floral prints, often quite bold. The ubiquity of flowers in both the dresses' printed patterns and the aprons' embroidery echoes how common flowers are on the traditional huipiles.

The two aprons we see Isabel Gutierrez wearing illustrate the wide variety available within the broad profile described in the previous paragraph. Craft salespersons like her, although usually better off than their contemporaries dressed similarly in public markets, work the same very long hours in the same dusty or grimy settings as do sellers of vegetables. Since Gutierrez's family is prosperous in working-class Mexican context, and since crafts are the family business—indeed, there's a sturdy sewing machine owned within the extended family—she has the time, materials, and certainly the ability to make aprons, but she says it makes more sense to buy them. However, each one is "to her taste," she quickly insists. And I've never seen two that were exactly alike in any

Figure 33. In Mérida and throughout the Yucatán Peninsula, simple aprons made with checked cloth are the rule. This photo, taken a four-hour bus ride away from Mérida in the public market in Campeche, also illustrates the simpler type of shopping bag sold throughout Mexico, made of nylon mesh in a variety of colors and simple striped or checked patterns.

apron maker's stand in any market. Though it is logical to have this be a specialists' craft, each buyer meets the maker and may be picky while selecting her personal apron. The one Gutierrez wears in figure 32 is as close to a meat-and-potatoes Oaxacan apron as I have ever seen her wear, while the far fancier one in figure 19 is as elaborate as can be found with any frequency in the state.

There are substyles of these aprons, sometimes simply makers' styles, since a substantial number of customers can be served by one busy seamstress. The main apron seamstress in Tlacolula—a bigger town than Teotitlán, about ten miles farther from Oaxaca down the same highway—embroiders more extravagantly than do the main makers in Oaxaca. Although Teotitlán is closer to Tlacolula than to the city of Oaxaca, more aprons of the city of Oaxaca substyle are seen in Teotitlán, largely owing to community taste. But differences between substyles are minor. And the general Oaxaca apron profile holds for hundreds of miles in every direction. I saw plenty of these aprons down south in Juchitán de Zaragoza, which is still in the state of Oaxaca, but nearly halfway from the city of Oaxaca to San Cristóbal. Aprons differ much less from community to community within the state of Oaxaca than do traditional ceremonial clothes or, for that matter, than do typical exemplars of *any* genre of craft items made for tourists today.

In striking contrast, in Mérida, market women's aprons are simpler in construction and decoration and are less a routine part of market dress. There they are straightforward pull-over-your-head and tie-on-sides rectangles with curved ends in a standard checked cloth (white and either some primary color or black). Many of them incorporate a fold in front that is sewn to make pockets to hold change, as in figure 33. The checks are a standard size (about one-quarter of an inch, a size of check used only for aprons), and embroidery is very rare. These are a practical accessory, not a locus for creativity or individual preference, beyond choosing the color of the checks. This type of apron dominates throughout the Yucatán Peninsula—the photo is in fact not from Mérida but from the public market in Campeche, on the Gulf Coast about 120 miles west of Mérida (and in the state of Campeche rather than Yucatán). Indeed, this relatively plain style of apron is just as geographically widespread as is the Oaxaca type.

Between the Yucatán and Oaxaca, in the mountains of Chiapas, we find the widest variety in apron construction. One sees many Oaxaca-type aprons, but some women consider them unsuitable. In San Cristóbal and environs, many Indian women never wear manufactured, store-bought dresses and are reluctant to cover their handmade traditional clothes, despite the practical advantages of aprons. Some women go without, some use Oaxaca types, and some compromise by wearing just a waist-and-down, front-only apron. Choices seem to be personal but correspond somewhat to group identity. Women originally from the nearby municipality of Chamula, but now living in slums around San Cristóbal, seem especially insistent on showing their traditional Indian dress and thus go without aprons. There is a partly religious factor here that I discuss in the next section.

### Slogans and Names Painted on Vehicles

An affluent Mexican man may mark his status through the make, model, and shiny newness of the car he drives. Poorer men may instead paint a few words on the modest, often group-owned or group-used vehicle they operate. This custom descends from an older practice: formerly, some men might have *dichos* (sayings) incised on their swords. That custom persists, especially on farmers' machetes. However, most of today's fancy knives bearing dichos are small and are marketed to tourists. Sayings on Oaxaca knives that I saw for sale in 2007 bore Oaxacan maxims, including the following, which I list with approximate translations. The dichos are deliberately witty and thus hard to get right in English:

Soy amigo de los hombres y azote de los traidores.
I'm a friend of [honorable] men, but I beat up on traitors.

Lo prometido es dueda si el que promete se acuerda.
That which is promised is owed only if the debtor remembers.

El que tiene buena mujer pop le queda por ver.
One who has a good woman has little left to see [does not need to look elsewhere].

Figure 34. Although second-class buses are assembled in factories, they are usually personally decorated with additions in the inside (air fresheners featuring cartoon characters and the Virgin of Guadalupe may hang side by side). Many buses also accumulate mottoes painted on the outside. Here a driver characterizes his bus as his "old friend" and "accomplice."

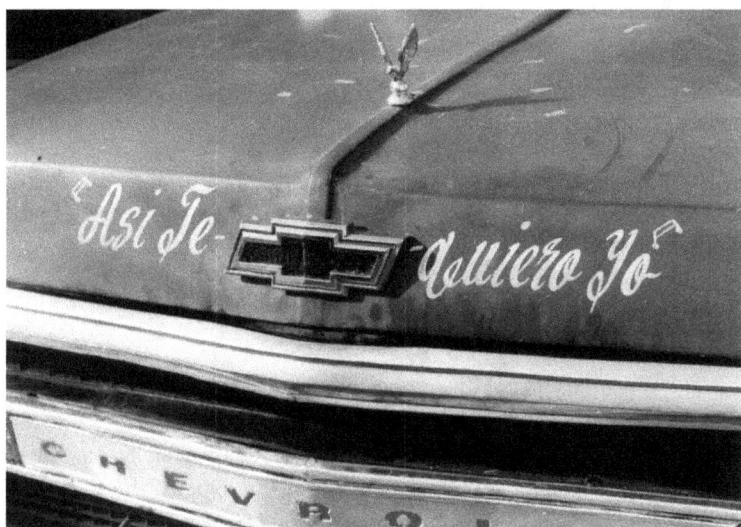

Figure 35. The song lyric "Asi te quiero yo" (That's the way I love you) decorates the hood of a pickup truck, offering a mood diametrically opposed to that of one of my favorite sayings painted on a Oaxaca city bus: "Arrepinter . . ." (Repent before it is too late).

Figure 36. Two manifestations of the Mother Mary—her various forms are treated as somewhat separate saints in Mexico's semi-polytheistic rural adjustments of Catholicism—on a truck from Zinacantan transporting fruit, flowers, and workers to San Cristóbal. The picture is of the Virgin of Guadalupe, Mexico's favorite national Mother Mary, and "Juquilita" is a diminutive for the Virgin of Juquila, who is widely worshiped in the South; both are brown-skinned Virgins.

Si de mi filo provaras de mi te acordaras.
You'd remember me if you tasted the edge of my blade.

Mala pal' metate pero buena pal' petate [petate = a woven mat].
[She is] not very industrious, but good in bed.

Soy como el camaleon chiquito pero cabrón.
I'm like a chameleon—small but a stud.

Today words and sayings are painted on the similarly masculine metal of vehicles—not as frequently on personal cars, however, as on personalized public transportation: buses, taxis (especially *colectivos*, i.e., intercity taxis and vans), and family pickup trucks, the ones that convey produce and workers to market. In Oaxaca, inscriptions are painted especially on trucks and on second-class intercity and city buses (those two functions tend to overlap, since the long-haul second-class buses also pause at city bus stops while approaching or leaving bus stations). There are a few sayings in the collective style of the ones on the knives now made for tourists, but those tend to be too long to fit well on vehicles; the usual viewing situation favors shorter inscriptions (see figures 34–35). More common than maxims are assertive nicknames. Every city seems to have a few buses labeled "Depredador" (the Terminator), which, in one word, projects an assertive, manly effect parallel to that underlying many of the sayings inscribed on knives. In contrasting approaches, some proud fathers list their children's names, and other men make compact religious statements. In Mérida, words are often painted on taxis and colectivos and on city buses—the emphasis is on kids' names here. But overall the practice is sparser and the inscriptions less varied there than in Oaxaca.

In and around San Cristóbal, we encounter about the same number of decorated vehicles per capita as in Oaxaca, but these feature a special emphasis on religious sayings and religious images placed on a particular kind of truck, the half-ton Nissan with quilted aluminum box. I reproduce a photo of one of these (figure 36), that is, a close-up of the box that extends right above the windshield. There is usually quite a bit of information packed in that space above the cab. You might see, for instance, a "Gracias a ti, Señor" painted across the bottom, a picture of one of the favorite manifestations of the Mother Mary where you see one here, and maybe an outline of Jesus' face above in that diamond. The truck in the photo references two Virgins—her various forms are treated as separate saints in Mexico's semi-polytheistic rural adjustments of Catholicism. The picture is of the Virgin of Guadalupe, Mexico's favorite national Mother Mary, and "Juquilita" is a diminutive for the Virgin of Juquila, who is widely worshiped in the south. She is, in fact, the most popular Virgin among most southern Mexican Indian populations. Her statue stands in a church in the mountains of Oaxaca: Juquila is a remote village and pilgrimage destination (and, incidentally, a frequent contributor of dance troupes to the Guelaguetza).

Decorated trucks can be seen most anywhere on any day in San Cristóbal. However, many of them go home at night to Zinacantan, a nearby flower- and vegetable-producing Mayan municipality. I return now to the religious factor I mentioned at the end of the previous section: many women who sell crafts in San Cristóbal's market moved to

**Table 5**

**Words and Sayings Painted on Buses, Trucks, and Cars in Oaxaca, San Cristóbal, and Mérida**

| Oaxaca | |
|---|---|
| Dichos (sayings) or catchy phrases | La Vida es un Sueño (life is a dream)<br>Nunca digas nunca (never say never)<br>El Privilegio de Amor (the privileges of love; a song title)<br>Viva México, Cabrones y no! FUI AL NORTE (Viva Mexico, fuckers: I didn't make it north)<br>Si de Dios Hablan de mi que diran (If they criticize God, what do they say about me?) |
| Religious sayings and references | Fe en Dios (faith in God)<br>Dios Mediante (by the grace of God)<br>En el Nombre de Dios (in the name of God)<br>Mitzy Juquila (one name, then one reference to the Virgin of Juquila) |
| Names and nicknames with attitude | Daniela Alexandra<br>Frederick<br>Piel Canela (cinnamon skin, presumably of a sweetheart)<br>Gitano Sonador (gypsy dreamer) |
| San Cristóbal | |
| Dichos (sayings) or catchy phrases | Frente al Destino (facing destiny; coupled with "Gracias a Dios")<br>Dios se Perdona, el Tiempo no (God may forgive you, but time will not); most sayings here are religious, including, in addition to those below, Regalo de Dios (gift of God), Dios es Amor (God is love), etc. |
| Religious sayings and references | Virgen de Juquila Amparame (forgive me, Virgin of Juquila)<br>Gracias a ti, Señor (thank you, Lord)<br>Dios es mi Camino (God is guiding me)<br>Dios es de Todo (God is everything) |
| Names and nicknames with attitude | Dennis (multiple names, suggesting a batch of kids, are rare here)<br>Xiomara (a common Nahuatl name)<br>El Troquero (the trucker)<br>Chico Malo (bad boy) |
| Mérida | |
| Dichos (sayings) or catchy phrases | 100% Fresa (100% clean [of drugs])<br>Corazon de Piedra (heart of stone: could as easily have been listed under names; few phrases as painted on vehicles here) |
| Religious sayings and references | El Sagrado Corazón de Jesus (the sacred heart of Jesus)<br>Dios es mi Juez (God is my judge; religious sayings aren't common here) |
| Names and nicknames with attitude | Ana Christina María Mariana<br>Odethe * María * Andres * Denis<br>Juan José Erica Adrian<br>Didier Omar (there are many citizens of Lebanese descent in Mérida)<br>www.juani.pauli.ricky (Mérida is more modern than the other two towns)<br>El Indomable (the wild one; "indomable" means "can't be domesticated")<br>The Black Demon (every once in a while, you see a name or phrase in English) |

the city from Chamula and still wear their traditional clothes. They do so because they prefer to remain Indian in both behavior and appearance rather than to adopt town ways and become acculturated Ladinos. In Chamula, the forbidding costs of supporting local Catholicism in an increasingly unwieldy cargo system had helped push a sizable fraction of the populace toward converting to evangelical Protestantism; but after conversion, thousands of new Protestants were exiled and moved to slums on the outskirts of San Cristóbal. They had wanted to change how they lived in Chamula, not leave town, and they still consider themselves Chamulans. Their sticking to traditional clothes—interfering with apron use—signals that identity. The residents of nearby Zinacantan are proud that they remained Catholic, and trumpet their pride all over the state through truck decoration. In short, the marked differences in recent history between these neighboring Indian towns in Chiapas are signaled in contrasting use of visible and portable traditional material culture. I should also note that many of these trucks are exceptionally well traveled. The Zinacantecos market flowers over a wide area, selling so many that they exceed the supply they grow and must buy more in central Mexico (Collier 1994, 150). Some trucks that make that long trip stop off in Oaxaca at the mountain shrine of Juquila, thus incorporating a short pilgrimage into a business journey (see figure 36).

Table 5 illustrates some of the words and sayings painted on vehicles in Oaxaca, San Cristóbal, and Mérida. Each of three basic topics is evident in such inscriptions in each city, but the emphases differ. Some paintings straddle categories, of course.

### Nylon and Plastic Shopping Baskets

Most shoppers in the markets carry their purchases in sturdy shopping baskets. You never see these baskets in grocery stores or malls; members of the middle and upper classes look down on these baskets. But they are practical in the big public markets, where shoppers walk in crowded aisles where shopping carts would not fit (besides, who would pay for those carts?). A nationally distributed type of bag is made of nylon mesh, with handles riveted on, like those pictured hanging above the produce saleswoman from Campeche in figure 33. I asked in markets in several

Figure 37. Three prison-made baskets. The leftmost one, made from plastic strings and ribbons in stake-and-strand weaving technique, represents the main type for sale in the state of Oaxaca (see also figure 44). The lattice type in the middle, woven from plastic ribbons and generally featuring a prominent cross-within-diamond design (as here), was the most popular with older Indian women merchants for many years, but the even stronger type such as the one on the left became more popular by 2002. The rightmost basket represents a younger practice of making baskets in prisons in Chiapas, a more time-consuming technique of using only slender plastic strings (not also the plastic ribbons that allow faster work in Oaxaca's jails).

cities where these bags were made, and was always given the name of some other big city or Mexico City. This type of bag is pretty much all you see in the markets in the north and is the only type in common use throughout the Yucatán. They are sold in every large market in Mexico and come in a riotous variety of plaids and stripes, so that shoppers can feel they're getting something somewhat distinctive and personal.

These mesh bags are supplemented in the state of Oaxaca and in San Cristóbal with more costly but "más durable" woven baskets (figure 37). These are made of special plastic strings and plastic ribbons in men's prisons, where inmates are encouraged to do work in designated handicrafts, ones that might not constitute economically sound activity outside. The prisoners make hammocks in many southern Mexican prisons, furniture in some, and also these shopping baskets in Oaxaca and now in upland Chiapas. They use what weavers call "stake-and-strand" construction, or "wickering." The bottom and sides of the basket are made of a framework of, in the case of rectangular baskets, straight segments of relatively rigid material interwoven with more pliable material passing over and under the stiff material, building up from the bottom. This is an old and widespread technique, one already in use in the late Bronze Age (Wright 1992, 175). The rectangular profile of the shopping baskets suits the narrow corridors in markets. In Oaxaca we see thin stakes and thicker, ribbonlike strands, while in Chiapas it's all thin material, and the baskets typically divide into three vertical panels rather than two. In both states there is also the same minority report, a slightly less durable and less costly checkerboard type (in Oaxaca, made in a different prison from the usual local type).

Just as in the cases of the aprons and the vehicle adornments, so shopping baskets achieve their most luxuriant variety in San Cristóbal. There are more kinds of plain plastic bags than found anywhere else in Mexico, a few nylon mesh bags with stenciled pictures of Frida Kahlo or Diego Rivera (for the odd European tourist venturing into the market, I suppose—I never saw any of those bags sold). And there are two different color schemes for handwoven bags crafted by prisoners, one with a base tone of beige (thus imitating straw or reed baskets; see the right side in figure 37) and one with more color options. Thus the regional penchant for great variety we already witnessed in the aprons and the truck decorating has quickly infused this more recently coalesced craft.

But it is in Oaxaca city that such shopping baskets have made their single successful foray into the tourist sphere. When Zapotec Indians from Loxicha were encamped on the square, they successfully sold baskets made by their imprisoned men, despite the "inauthentic" plastic materials employed (figure 43). I believe that some tourists who bought these—Americans and Europeans did so, but not Mexican visitors— were willing to overlook the synthetic raw materials because they could assuage their liberal or radical politics through these purchases. These tourists bought these products steadily only until the Loxicha were shunted away from the square to a dingy apartment a few blocks north. I visited the remnants of that group and was told that basket sales ceased as soon as the Indians ceased to be as visible. A Oaxacan mestizo entrepreneur tried to sell some of these baskets in New York. There seems to have been a tiny but real market for them, and for a year or two, all-black or silver versions were in style among some women in New York who could thus be politically interesting and chic at the same time. He said that the fashion soon faded, just as one trend in fashionable politics would yield to another.

What general observations did I make about these three categories of "new traditional" material culture? First, concerning the markets themselves: Unsurprisingly, the more grounded in tradition the area—and the lower the per capita income—the larger the markets were per capita. I made a point of visiting markets in a few prosperous northern cities on my way to Oaxaca in July 2007. The downtown public market in Monterrey is smaller than that in Saltillo, which is smaller than that in Mérida; all of these are smaller when adjusted per capita than those in Oaxaca and Chiapas. The overall vitality of the three sorts of traditional genres of material culture I looked at for this chapter is quite congruent with the size of the markets, too—the bigger the markets per capita, the more varied and interesting the associated material culture.

These three arrays of tradition-generated objects not directed toward tourists do share certain characteristics. They illustrate a pleasantly old-fashioned balancing of personal creativity and regional gravitational fields in both conception and making. Geographic variation does persist, with some change in how that works. Traditional things and practices cluster in physically larger geographic areas than before, but those areas are not bigger in another sense, that of how long it takes to get from here to there. That is, in terms of travel time rather than absolute distance, the new, larger "tradition turfs" are quite comparable to the smaller ones of previous eras.

Last, I compared these traditions with tourist crafts in terms of density of visual effect. Various kinds of folkloric intensification commonplace in the tourist crafts—aesthetic processes that come into play to replace lost functions—either are absent in these community traditions or respond to new cultural factors. For instance, the neighboring municipalities of Zinacantan and Chamula in the highlands of Chiapas have different recent religious histories, and that difference is reflected in the Zinacantecos' frequent decoration of pickup trucks in a manner that is both artistically extravagant and somewhat confrontational. How, in general, did the objects look? Tradition-generated objects outside the tourist sphere tend to be brighter in color than are many tourist crafts (perhaps in part because there is no worry about natural dyes), and tend to involve an unselfconscious mix of old and new raw materials. The craftsmen are not worrying about the letter of authenticity; they are embodying its spirit.

### Tiro al Blanco: A Marksmanship and Music Game at Carnivals

When the Christmas season, the fortnight of the Guelaguetza, or any other festive time approaches, Oaxaca is gradually transformed. Carnival booths accumulate across from the cathedral and extend down neighboring streets for a block in several directions. Market stands, games of skill, and creaky old rides proliferate wildly and remain in business for the duration of the festivities. The more generic carnival booths in Oaxaca include the routine semirigged contests, snacks (tacos, pancakes, seasonal pastries), and displays of cheap jewelry and similar small, optional purchases. One test of skill stands out. Tiro al blanco is an unusual combination of shooting gallery and jukebox, and of traditional and modern popular culture. I discuss it at length here because it can stand for many aspects of festivals, ingredients that, like aprons, car decorations, and baskets, are little noticed by tourists. Thus the tiro al blanco game constitutes one of many small, "background-noise" parallels to the Guelaguetza in roughly the same way that the aprons, slogans, and baskets are barely visible and economically insignificant counterparts to the tourist-oriented pottery, weavings, and carvings of chapters 1 and 2.

In a typical tiro al blanco setup, over a dozen rows of tiny metal targets flank a series of alcoves modeled on the little instructive scenes (*retablos*) common in churches. Each rectangular display contains a set of mechanically animated figures, in most cases musical groups, but in others Day of the Dead figurines (see figure 38). While the large metal skeleton in front of the game refers to the popular movie *The Terminator*—as the skeleton leans left and right at unpredictable intervals, his machine gun sprays water on passersby to add a fillip of danger to

Figure 38. A common carnival game called tiro al blanco. The participant aims at small metal figures, rows of which are seen on the right, or selects specific targets in a central panel. Hitting one of these smaller, more difficult targets wins the animation and playing of music from recordings by a musical group represented by puppets in a glass case. Most of these ensembles perform conservative genres, especially norteña, banda, and ranchera (mariachi). If the target linked to the skeletal Day of the Dead figurines is hit, rock music blares forth. Also, the large skeleton (a Day of the Dead figure? The Terminator? Both?) rotates and occasionally shoots water in a arc, wetting lots of contestants and onlookers.

the game and to advertise it to those within earshot of the consequent shrieks—the smaller skeletons echo the Day of the Dead retablos found in homes (and those sold to tourists).

In Mexico, many believe that the souls of the dead return to earth on November 1 and 2, All Saints' Day and All Souls' Day. Families enthusiastically celebrate, picnicking in graveyards and bringing small gifts for the departed. (One need not believe fervently in the souls' return to enjoy participating, just as in the United States one need not be ardently Christian or believe in Santa Claus to enjoy Christmas.) Special candies shaped like skeletons or skulls are made then, and memories of the day extend throughout the year through the crafting of little scenes of wooden, pottery, or metal skeletons taking part in daily life—visiting the drugstore or post office, dancing, eating a meal, or often, as in the game of tiro al blanco, playing music. Juxtaposing these singing skeletons with popular professional musical groups in these particular retablos is a concentrated example of the general flavor of any Mexican festival, that is, of pop culture and traditional religion mixing in casually delirious eclecticism. Indeed, the double meaning of skeletons in the game—that is, having the life-size *Terminator* skeleton just a few feet from the Day of the Dead miniatures—highlights both this marriage and its eclecticism.

The tiro al blanco game echoes tradition in several additional ways. Marksmanship is an old-fashioned skill, one needed more day to day in the past than present, but still having practical value in the countryside, and still central to the generalized Mexican male self-image. And the retablos are mechanized. As songs play, the figures move, visually recalling the ubiquitous puppet shows of the past. In most carnival games, a competitor can win a stuffed toy or other modest tangible prize. In tiro al blanco, the marksman who hits one of the most difficult targets (see the upper left in the photo, above the Tigres del Norte retablo) gets a different and fleeting reward, part of a song from one of the bands in the retablos. Hitting a given target trips the switch for a specific ensemble.

If a tiro al blanco game is to produce profits, the performers represented in the little scenes must be ones that carnival-goers wish to hear. There are many genres of popular music in Mexico—indeed, quite a variety is heard by anyone visiting the city square on any given evening. But only a few of the multitude of popular singers and ensembles and, for that matter, musical styles can be featured in the game, so their choice is quite significant. This selection embodies a sort of insiders' core repertoire of performers and the specific genres of music that those performers represent. To understand why it is the poor who are the main patrons of this game, to explore how tradition infuses the music featured in it, and to demonstrate why this flourishing and fascinating genre of festival game does not interest tourists or affluent citizens of Mexico, I must digress to introduce Mexican popular music.

Music is an indispensable ingredient in even the hand-to-mouth existence of the poorest residents of southern Mexico. Radios or boom boxes blare in shabby second-class buses, and a day's labor in even the humblest of market stalls is eased by the companionship of recorded songs. Small televisions operate constantly in slightly upscale market stalls and in shops in poor parts of town, often showing rurally themed action films that are—despite being soaked in cordite—musicals, each built around a half-dozen songs. Indeed, most of the secular musical experiences that lower-class Mexicans—that is, most Mexicans—have are with commercial popular music, which, as part of its being popular, has been shaped and delivered by major corporations, the same half-dozen transnational entertainment conglomerates that dominate audiogram production and sales worldwide. Every one of the ensembles represented in any Oaxaca shooting gallery carnival game is signed, recorded, and distributed by one of these corporations.

Having a music-cultural complex administered by the mass media does not mean that tradition is erased from the music. In the lower rungs of Mexican popular music, we can find tradition surviving in a matrix of attitudes and practices retained (and revised) through flexible mixtures of conviction, stubbornness, and inertia, interacting with a complementary array of evolving needs—attitudes and practices that both reflect and continually reshape critical cultural values. I believe that this process lies behind which musicians are featured in the Oaxaca shooting gallery carnival game, and does so as part of a double-barreled cultural diplomacy: between past and present and between inherited socioeconomic station and ambition.

One can rank genres of Mexican pop music on a socioeconomic ladder simply by noting which genres please which groups of people. But these preferences reach beyond patterns of purchases into all kinds of associated behavior, which end up being entry points for tradition. As is true throughout Latin America, many types of nationally distributed music were once local repertoires in terms of both production and reception. As of this writing, Mexico's main popular music genres (as defined in stores, over the radio, and in conversation) are, starting from rural or regionally based lowbrow and progressing through the socioeconomic spectrum to urban middlebrow: *norteña, banda, ranchera, tropical, balada, moderna* or *pop*, and English language (moderna and *inglés* overlap with rock and rap). Today there still is a rough correlation between socioeconomic affiliation of genres and the degree to which their origins can be pinpointed geographically. The first four genres listed, the lowest-brow ones, were originally intimately regional, while the remaining three bear less precise geographic affiliations.

Musíca norteña, the lowest-ranked commercially viable music, comes from the broad northern reaches of Mexico, from the mountains and deserts and mining areas that nurtured the revolution of 1910. This genre centers on *corridos* (narrative ballads of the revolution, illegal migration of wetbacks or *mojados*, the narcotics trade, and so forth); *rancheras* (rural love songs) for one or several singers who accompany themselves on accordion, guitar, often bass, and sometimes saxophone in polka or waltz meters; and *cumbias norteñas* (with rhythms borrowed from the genre known as tropical, but retaining norteña lyrics and core instrumentation; also sometimes called *tropi-norteña*). A newer, sociologically affiliated genre, *banda*, in which a singer is accompanied by a wind band, represents a recent flowering into the popular sphere of widespread community band styles, especially as these crystallized in Sinaloa, on the west coast (Simonett 2001). The banda repertoire largely parallels that of norteña, though with a young rapid duple-time dance called the *quebradita* emphasized. The category of ranchera, today roughly synonymous with mariachi music, comes originally from Guadalajara and the surrounding state of Jalisco, east and south of Mexico City. This genre includes additional rancheras—and many other songs and tunes—in performances marked by more vocal drama and slightly higher production values. The salsa relative called tropical centers on cumbias, from the steamy, cosmopolitan gulf coast of Veracruz (though reflecting pan-Caribbean influence, with the Mexican cumbia itself especially influenced by the cumbias of Colombia). Tropical joins disco and watered-down rap in discotheques nationwide but has also retained primary lower-class associations since its introduction in the middle of the twentieth century (Stigberg 1978, 277). Genres higher on the socioeconomic ladder—*romántica* (or balada), pop/moderna, and rock, are progressively more international in sound and popularity.

Poor people's favorite music genres' regional origins are still marked by how performers dress, particularly the similarly cowboy-oriented yet distinctively stylized outfits worn by performers of norteña, banda, and ranchera. These genres have other things in common. Woman performers are statistically rarer here than in higher-ranked genres. Musical language tends to be highly compact, especially in norteña. Singers express text especially clearly, which is a tiny symptom of an important feature of Mexican pop music consumption: minimizing the passiveness of reception, shrinking the gulf between performer and audience. For instance, when mariachis or other *ambulantes* (the generic term for strolling professional musicians) work restaurants or bars, honoring requests for a few dollars per song, a tune's requestor often will sing along. At all types of concerts, audience members sing along with hits from all genres. This is facilitated by performers' crisp diction, compact musical language, manageably sized core repertoires, and a strong tradition of participation. Also, the closer we go to the lowbrow end, the more cuts are covers, and the more songs were once in public domain, so that record companies, rather than the forgotten composers and lyricists, hold the copyrights (fully a third of older norteña recordings).

Many norteña and banda recordings are like unrehearsed performances using musical means the general populace can at least imagine commanding. Indeed, the poorest peasants, Indians, listen most to norteña, with its unaffected vocal delivery, accordions (sounding not unlike the harmonicas they can afford), and guitars (and even occasionally violins), which are similar to instruments that many Indian communities make. Norteña is certainly the primary music of the Indians of Oaxaca. This surprised me initially and is denied by some middle-class Oaxacans: on two separate occasions, elegantly dressed and elaborately coiffed managers of music stores in a prosperous northern section of Oaxaca acted as if they found my question "Do you sell much norteña?" exceptionally ignorant. "Norteña is from the North: it's played and sold only there," one told me with a carefully neutral look that silently appended: "you cretinous tourist." However, I found that in stores and cassette and CD stands on the other side of downtown Oaxaca, on the bus station-to-market axis, norteña was second in sales only to tropical. In the Indian villages surrounding Oaxaca, craftsmen and craftswomen make objects with venerable antecedents, now stylized for tourists, while listening to norteña cassettes or CDs.

Why norteña so far south? The Zapotec rug maker Felipe Hernández told me that it was because of the lyrics, which in corridos often describe social unrest. Many Indians, including many Zapotecs from the valley of Oaxaca, fought in the revolution, not so many generations ago. Few of the changes they fought for have taken place, and turmoil never recedes far below the surfaces of their lives. Today half or more of the men in many villages are forced to migrate north to find work. They hear norteña there and are attracted to it, at least partly due to their economic plight. Felipe's favorite group is Los Tigres del Norte, an old-fashioned group within that old-fashioned genre. Today's norteña has largely replaced the corridos about the revolution with ones about border crossing and, most recently, *narcocorridos* celebrating the kingpins of the illegal but hugely profitable drug trade. What these topics have in common is the joining of the morally or legally ambiguous activities with an emphasis on men behaving in a manly way, despite their being embroiled in circumstances that are perilous, demeaning, or both.

CDs and tapes in the lowest-ranked genres are sold at stands and in scruffy little stores along what one might call a city's "internal rural routes," that is, broad lines drawn between the second-class out-of-town bus station (usually located on the outer edge of the commercial part of town), main open-air market, and town square, which houses the twin necessities of cathedral and bandstand. Those broad lines that the poor walk regularly within the cities take on a special character, becoming extensions of their villages in many ways. These lines of country-within-city are especially easy to trace in Oaxaca. The enormous second-class bus station lies just to the east of the *periférico* (the multilane road circling the mercantile center of the city). Across from the station's entrance begins the labyrinth of the newer and larger of the open-air markets, over a square mile of stalls. About ten blocks due east (straight into town) is the older market, a roofed complex of two square blocks; the city zócalo—actually several linked wooded blocks—is two blocks north of this older market. Thus the internal rural routes of Oaxaca include a line from west to town center of about twelve blocks (actually two parallel lines, since two streets are equally convenient) and a shorter leg extending two blocks north, again on two equally walked parallel streets. Why do so many rural citizens take the bus *to* a metropolis, then rarely use the city buses? This choice is a matter of keeping small costs at a minimum: a ticket of, say, a half-dollar will bring a person (and bags of produce or crafts and a hand truck) from village to city, an impractical distance of tens of kilometers if the traveler is on foot, while it might cost another fifteen cents to traverse the kilometer (or less) from bus station to market, a distance that can be walked in under an hour, even by those heavily laden.

The range of Mexican popular music genres—and of their audiences—is matched by a continuum of attitudes and behavior ranging from trendy to traditional. On one end are moderna and rock, media propelled and technology dependent, with rapid turnover and distinctive songs performed by stars, sold (especially on CDs) to affluent, internationally oriented youth. At the other extreme are norteña and banda, performed easily (with minimal expense and training), with the highest public-domain quotient, most traditional topics, and least striving for musical novelty, sold in public markets and along each city's internal rural routes in the form of cassettes or CDs (often pirated) to the poor, who resist the blandishments of radio and advertising to retain old genres and old ways. The mass music machine churns energetically in Mexico but has failed to sever a variety of links between tradition and the nature and consumption of popular music.

With this considerable list of ways in mind that tradition influences—indeed, lives on in—the consumption of commercial popular music in Mexico, the initially striking nature of the Oaxacan shooting gallery carnival stand in which skilled marksmanship wins a song becomes less surprising. Here is a complete list of the popular music ensembles presented in this particular tiro al blanco game, with the genre of music that the groups play. I will name each rectangle, whether a retablo of musicians or a section of target, starting at the top left of the game, reading across, then from the bottom left, reading across again; only the right side of the game is visible in this photograph.

| | |
|---|---|
| Vicente y Alejandro Fernandez | ranchera/mariachi(Vicente is movie star, too) |
| Mi Banda El Mexicano | banda (*technobanda*, i.e., uses some electronics) |
| Los Tucanes de Tijuana | norteña (old-fashioned within the genre) |

(targets for each musical group: if you hit one, you hear a song or part of one)

| | |
|---|---|
| Ritmo Duranguense | norteña (if broadly understood; newish) |
| Caballo Dorado | a cover dance band for American Country hits |
| Intocable | norteña |

(a broad rectangle containing general targets: rows of ships, ducks, etc.)

| | |
|---|---|
| Recodo Banda | banda; old-fashioned, like a village wind  band |
| Tigres del Norte | norteña (old-fashioned) |

(day of the dead figures, which play raucous rock music with a classic rock feel)
(the other broad rectangle of general targets)

Of the genres illustrated by mechanized puppets of real musical en-sembles, the highest ranked in socioeconomic terms is ranchera, repre-sented here by Vicente Fernandez and his son Alejandro. Vicente, born in 1940, explored other professions before becoming a professional singer and singing actor. In the last thirty years, he has starred in many movies and made nearly twice as many recordings. He is the most fa-mous living ranchera singer and most famous star of movies featuring rancheras. He (and his son, with whom he occasionally collaborates) are photographed for album covers wearing *charro* clothing, the stylized garb associated with cowboys—that is, affluent Mexican ranch own-ers of the past—the same type of outfit that mariachi musicians have as their uniform. He appeals up and down the socioeconomic ladder due to his fame as an actor.

The group Caballo Dorado appeals especially to the many Mexican men who have worked in the United States and may have had better access to live performances of American country and western than to any live Mexican music while in the United States. Caballo Dorado's repertoire centers on country songs popular for line dancing; this music is less for listening than for participation.

The remaining artists and ensembles all belong to the enormous norteña or banda groups, both genres that have old-fashioned and somewhat more progressive ends, with these subgenres of both repre-sented at this tiro al blanco game. This combination of some measured modernization (and performers' economic success) with tradition-ori-ented genres and behavior suggests a parallel portrait of poor Mexican men, of their desire to better themselves financially without abandoning family, machismo, and other enduring values. At the same time, the basic meters and tempos of most of the music played at the tiro al blanco game echo the oldest combinations of regularly heard traditional music in Oaxaca, the waltzes, polkas, and sones played by wind or string bands back in the municipalities, the same types of tunes heard at the Guelaguetza.

Thus the music of the tiro al blanco festival game, drawing overwhelmingly on the most traditional of Mexican popular music genres, mixes modern means and materials with traditional attitudes in ways similar to how these factors mesh in the genres of modern traditional folk objects discussed earlier in the chapter. The baskets are handwoven in traditional shapes out of modern plastic or nylon. The aprons are useful garments crafted individually, with the old theme of flowers embroidered by machine on purchased mass-produced cloth. And sayings related to those once incised on swords are now painted on modern trucks and buses. These genres casually bridge the past and present, just as does the tiro al blanco game. Pursuing the spirit of tradition by drawing on the most readily available materials and means of distribution, even when the modernity of these violates the letter of historical authenticity, suits the spirit of tradition. In short, some of the very aspects of the new traditional genres that tourists do not support financially are the very aspects that avoid the ruptures in the spirit of tradition that characterize the tourist-oriented crafts and festivals, those that obey the letter more than the spirit of tradition and are much younger than their purchasers or audiences would like to think.

Are the genres analyzed in this chapter exceptional or part of a broad tendency to find ways to cultivate tradition around the edges of mass culture? I briefly cite a few other examples of new traditional crafts, these affiliated with the general ethos or specific practical needs of festivity. First are handmade hats once sold at the Guelaguetza. These hats are not needed today, since cheap straw sombreros are passed out to all in the inner circle of paying seats. However, in the 1990s, before cheap sombreros became Guelaguetza party favors for the paying audience, entrepreneurial craftsmen made colorful folding hats by recycling thin cardboard cases that had held foodstuffs or powdered household clean-

Figure 39. New crafts respond to new materials and new opportunities, both in festivals and in daily life. At the Guelaguetza during the 1990s, audience members who forgot to bring hats could purchase umbrella-like folding headgear pieced together from light cardboard boxes that had once contained candy or, as here, detergent. In a parallel temporary festival-serving craft, such boxes were combined with small pieces of mirror to make fragile but serviceable periscopes, useful in situations when it is difficult to see over other audience members (for example, in the standing room for the Plaza de la Danza, near downtown Oaxaca).

ers. If one did not look too closely, the brand names receded from perception, leaving just pleasant patterns (see figure 39; figure 42 shows a nonfestival use of the same sorts of recycled boxes). In a parallel temporary festival-serving craft, such boxes are combined with small pieces of mirror to make fragile but serviceable periscopes, useful in situations when it is difficult to see over other audience members (for example, in the standing room at the Plaza de la Danza, near downtown Oaxaca).

Not specific to any particular festival but always projecting a happy mood are balloons. I have never seen so many in one place as on the Oaxaca zócalo on most evenings. Each vendor shepherds many dozens of inflated balloons in a giant bouquet. Most are commercial products, but a significant minority begin life as straightforward translucent balloons, to which the seller adds facial features with magic markers and

Figure 40. Balloons and balloon-based toys also suit a festival mood (cheerful but temporary). On many evenings, over a dozen vendors line parts of the Oaxaca city square. Their wares include cylindrical balloons several meters long and about 20 cm thick, which one wallops to send high in the air, and also balloons with painted faces such as the girls and octopus shown here.

Figure 41. The balloon toys made in Oaxaca do not appear in Chiapas, where, instead, puppies elaborately crafted from balloons are ubiquitous in some years. These have bottle caps as feet and so can be "walked" loudly.

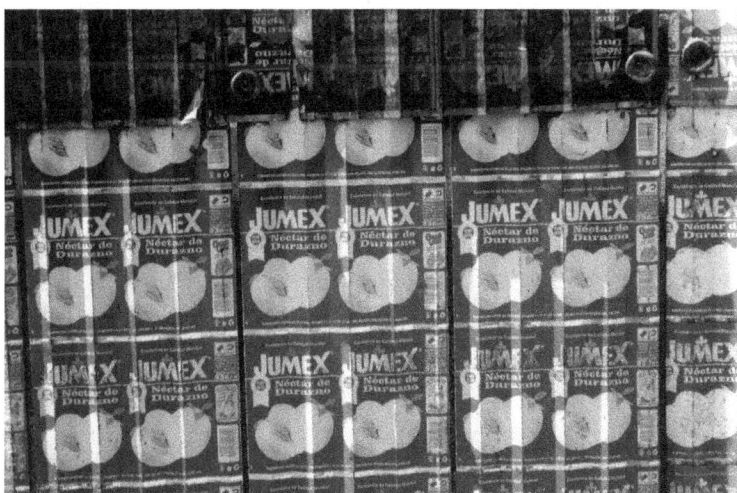

Figure 42. Thin metal cans for juice concentrates (here, Jumex peach punch) fastened to a fence to create a visual barrier. The labor is considerable, but the materials are free, and the results a visually pleasant patterned alternative to blank space.

attaches smaller balloons to represent the limbs of a doll or octopus or other temporary toy. Figure 40 shows these as commonly made in Oaxaca, while figure 41 illustrates the balloon puppies I see each time I visit San Cristóbal in Chiapas. In short, the traditional impulse to hand-make crafts or to add personal touches by hand to manufactured objects seems to be omnipresent in southern Mexico. These practices humanize mass culture and keep people in touch with their cultures' recent histories, and will continue to serve these functions whether or not tourists are around. At the same time, the enduring impulses supporting these practices constitute the psychological and cultural bedrock from which the tourist-serving crafts and festivals also spring.

# 5.

# Things Fall Apart: Attacks on Tourism in Oaxaca and the Prospects for Recovery

I hoped to go to Oaxaca in July 2006 to attend the Guelaguetza. I would find out if the festival continued to evolve or had reached a stable balance between the authenticity that tourists demand (however romantically and imprecisely) and the aesthetic intensification outsiders also favor without knowing they are doing so. I hoped to visit friends who wove rugs or carved and painted wooden figures for tourists and the international market, and to see how similar issues were playing out in their work. And I expected to evaluate how the parallel world of new traditional crafts *not* supported by tourists was evolving. But my trip was delayed and then took a surprising turn, because Oaxaca's long-term socioeconomic formula balancing poverty, authoritarian rule, and an economy reliant on ethnic tourism unraveled.

Before booking my flight, I caught up on the news from Oaxaca. I learned that the annual teachers' strike had been unusually large and protracted and was still escalating rather than resolving on schedule. I kept waiting to hear that the twenty-sixth consecutive strike had ended as had the first twenty-five, with a token raise and a return to the classroom. Instead confrontation led to violence, to gunfire, and to a climax that initially seemed bizarre—the Guelaguetza auditorium was vandalized just before the festival was scheduled to take place, and the event was canceled for the first time in decades. Dismayed, I canceled my travel plans. I wondered: Why attack the event that is the focus for both tradition and tourism in this part of the world? What might this mean for the future of Oaxaca?

## Oaxaca, 1990s–2006: A Fragile Peace Frays, and Hostility to Ethnic Tourism Grows

During visits to Oaxaca in 1995 and 1997, I had happened upon pro-test marches—or rather, these marches were routed through the central square, so that both affluent locals and tourists like me could not help but witness them. Years passed, and these two marches began to blend together in my memory. A few questions posed during later visits re-vealed why: the marches didn't just appear to be similar; they had the same purpose and included many of the same participants carrying the same sturdy signs. Teachers from throughout the state were publicizing that they were on strike. They wanted marginally better salaries and, es-pecially, money for basic classroom supplies such as books and candles. Moreover, in both years, teachers were joined by women in long huip-iles bearing lots of horizontal red stripes, women who I learned were members of the Triqui Indian population.

In fact, every year that the teachers struck and marched, their num-bers were reinforced by members of other disaffected groups, includ-ing the Triqui. Just as regularly, when the teachers received a minimal raise and returned to work, their allies in the protest disbanded too. But the summer of 2006 was different. Many citizens of Oaxaca were extremely unhappy with Governor Ulises Ruíz Ortíz, who took a hard line with protests and any social disquiet—he departed from custom by stonewalling the striking teachers—and whose 2004 election was widely perceived as blatantly fraudulent. The Mexican presidential elec-tion of 2006, also considered to have been more crooked than the norm, further fueled the rising level of discontent. Then these seething issues piggybacked on the teachers' strike, and—but I am getting ahead of my-self. Allow me to set the scene more thoroughly.

The essential ingredients in what would become a disastrous sum-mer for Oaxaca are deeply rooted in Mexican history. Throughout the state, but especially in the countryside, per capita incomes have always been tiny, glaringly so given how rich a few families are. Little money is allotted for public education and even less for other social services. Rural towns basically fend for themselves. Today families grow, but farms cannot. Indeed, due to clumsy deforestation and various agricultural blunders, the amount of productive arable land keeps shrinking. Some of the growing populace drains off through migration to slums of major cities; many villages exist both in one rural and in at least one urban location, as well as in dense traffic on the second-class buses joining those centers. And many men must migrate farther to work in the relatively prosperous north of Mexico or in the United States as illegal immigrants, as the mojados sung about in many recent norteña corridos. Perhaps half of the municipalities in Oaxaca depend on income sent home from such migrant workers, a steady stream of money that may even outweigh income earned through tourism (Caballero 2002; Espina 2002). Nevertheless farmland remains the key to village identity, and the scarcity of arable land in a time of unremitting population growth means that agrarian disputes boil over regularly.

Members of the Triqui have been visible on the square for decades, sometimes peddling weavings, but often just sleeping (though their main camp was in another park a few blocks north). Most of the Triqui who end up in the city of Oaxaca come from San Juan Copala, a community within the municipality of Juxtlahuaca in the Mixtec district of the state, near the border with Guerrero. Mixtec speakers surround the Triqui and look down on them. The Copala Triqui often cultivate coffee or bananas, while other, smaller, contiguous Triqui communities living at higher elevations settle for subsistence agriculture, mostly of corn and beans. Pressure from within and without—feuding based on agrarian disputes inside Triqui territory is endemic, and land snatching by surrounding populations has also been a regular feature of Triqui history—has produced waves of refugees.

Many immigrants to the city of Oaxaca from this especially poverty-stricken and violence-ridden part of the state have settled in the slums around the city, and a core group have become part of "zócalo culture," selling flowers, minor crafts, and even handwoven huipiles to tourists. For instance, Andrés Gutierrez Mendoza and his wife María Perez Santiago arrived in the city in an ambulance in 1988, after he was shot in the back accidentally in their home in San Juan Copala. He has since been

Figure 43. Women belonging to the Indian group called Triqui, from far western Oaxaca, wear indigenous dress regularly. Many of them now reside in Oaxaca city and are conspicuous because they constitute many of the flower saleswomen and crafts makers and sellers on the square. For instance, María Perez Santiago and her husband Andrés Gutierrez Mendoza make wristlets, headbands (my daughters still wear some of these), and personalized pens. They came to Oaxaca a dozen years ago, after a gunshot wound left Andrés confined to a wheelchair.

confined to a wheelchair. They walk (and wheel) in from their home several miles from downtown in an outlying colonia every day. They stake out their customary spot on the square and make wristlets, cover plastic headbands with colorful thread (see figure 43), and do the same to pens by the dozens. Their dream is (or was; I haven't seen them during my last few visits) to own a small piece of land and a few chickens.

Many other Triqui women and children are ambulatory sellers of the very cheapest wooden souvenirs, that is, simply carved letter openers and hot chocolate stirrers, both often infested with powder-post beetles. Last, during those festival times when more crafts than usual are for sale in temporary booths on the square, a dozen or so Triqui women peddle wall hangings and a few huipiles. They cater to tourist taste as well as they can, even making their huipiles in colors other than the traditional red to sell to outsiders. But the presence of these exotically dressed women and their children working on the square is not just one more sparkling tile in the ethnic mosaic of Oaxaca. They serve as a constant reminder that the Indians of Oaxaca's Valles Centrales (the central valleys), however humble their socioeconomic status may seem to visitors fresh off the plane, are doing stunningly well in their tourism-buttressed economy in comparison with most of the Indians of Oaxaca, such as the Triqui. The Triqui know this, resent it, and are always ready to join protests.

The longest-lasting recent encampment on the square was of women and children from San Agustín Loxicha. The Zapotec in the Loxicha area of rural southern Oaxaca numbered about thirty-five thousand before recent turmoil forced many to leave. Like many of the Triqui, most Indians in that region lack electricity, potable running water, regular access to medical care, and even the most basic educational opportunities. The Loxicha Zapotec experienced a long-running conflict with a half-dozen rich and powerful families who moved into San Agustín in the 1950s and became so-called caciques, controlling local access to all goods from outside. They ground down the Loxicha Zapotec into what amounted to a sharecropping economy, one in which the farmers were perpetually in debt due to the caciques' overpricing of essential supplies and ruinous loan rates. The rich families employed vicious paramilitary forces to maintain their control. Nevertheless the caciques and their henchmen were thrown out in 1978.

In late July 1996, a rebel force called the EPR (Ejército Popular Revolucionario, or Revolutionary People's Army) attacked police barracks in several locations, among them Huatulco, on Oaxaca's coast. On the basis of dubious evidence, this was blamed on the Indians of Loxicha. Many of the some 137 Loxicha men who were then taken into custody were community leaders—government officials and teachers—identified by former caciques who accompanied the army. The prisoners were tortured and signed confessions; eighty-six were still incarcerated in 2000. On June 10, 1997, a group of wives, children, and mothers of the prisoners arrived in Oaxaca and established an encampment of about thirty women and twenty children on the square that would last well into 2002 (a rotating group, but always about that size). For money, many of the women cleaned houses and washed clothes. They publicized the plight of their men on banners and on signs featuring the men's pictures (one portrait is barely visible on the left in figure 4). In 1998 the children, perhaps with some help from their mothers, painted the bright banner dominating figure 4. The longest statement painted on this panorama read, in not completely correct Spanish:

Mi papa esta en la carcel y ce emferma mucho y mi mamá no tiene dinero para comprar medecina y po eso estoy muy triste pues los policia agararon namas el es inocente ningun respuesta no nos a dado el gobierno Jose murat y po eso estamos en el Planton exigeindo La Libertad imediata a 96 preso de loxicha pero nosotros escribimos loxicha pero porque hade otro rancho y yo quiero mucho a mi papa pues nimodos policia lo hicot mi papá no tiene dinero para ni sus hijos a la escuela no tiene dinero yo me llame Ofelia Ambrocio Antonio.

[My father is in jail and gets sick often and my mother doesn't have money to buy medicine and that is why I am very sad because the police just snatched him and he is innocent no answer has been given by governor José Murat and that's why we're in the protest camp demanding immediate freedom for the 96 prisoners from Loxicha but we write [specify] Loxicha but because there are [some prisoners] from other villages and I love my dad very much but no matter what the police got him my dad has no money even to send his kids to school he has no money. My name is Ofelia [also signed] Ambrocio [and] Antonio.]

All other banners displayed by the Loxicha featured impeccable, educated spelling, phrasing, and punctuation; they were clearly composed by the teachers sympathetic to the protesters. This one really does seem to be a children's banner or at least one without much intervention by outside helpers. It radiates a youthful impetuousness, and *medecina* is a typical rural respelling of the conventional *medicina*. The banner attracted the attention of many more tourists who sympathized with the plight of the defenseless than did the signs painted by adults; perhaps these visitors remained wary of broader politics as exemplified in the more-educated banners. The Loxicha and their allies also offered passersby who appeared to be tourists from abroad a chance to help and to exercise their liberal politics by signing the following petition:

Governor Murat, I would much like to visit Oaxaca. However, I am very concerned that those responsible for the repression, assassinations, unjust incarcerations and torture of community leaders in Loxicha have not been brought to justice. I urge you to restore peace and justice to this community now.

But the most effective way that the families from Loxicha managed to draw the attention of tourists on the square to their plight was by selling eye-catching baskets made by their men while confined in Oaxaca's Santa María Ixcotel prison (a topic briefly introduced in the previous chapter; see figure 44). These baskets were made in an antic variety of colors right from the start. So many sold for a while that the families had to add baskets made by other prisoners in that jail to those woven by their own relatives. In addition, they catered to the group aesthetic preference of tourists from New York by also making their usual sizes and shapes of baskets in solid black or silver or gold; black sold best among those relatively austere options. Tourists who bought plastic baskets in their original colorful embodiments were sacrificing some of their preference for by-the-book authenticity—such baskets are, after all, not made from organic materials—because of the passionate political appeal. Then, when some of the baskets were black or silver, and thus more in tune with certain tourists' customary fashion accessories, so much the better. Also, other kinds of baskets were made, too, ones less

Figure 44. The long-term encampment of families from Loxicha on the square in Oaxaca was supported in large part through selling eye-catching baskets made by the men from Loxicha while confined in Oaxaca's Santa María Ixcotel prison. So many baskets sold during a brief efflorescence of politically conscious tourist enthusiasm that the families had to add baskets made by the miscellany of other prisoners in the jail to those woven by their own relatives. But the enduring sales of such baskets are to women who shop in Oaxaca's open-air markets, as shown here.

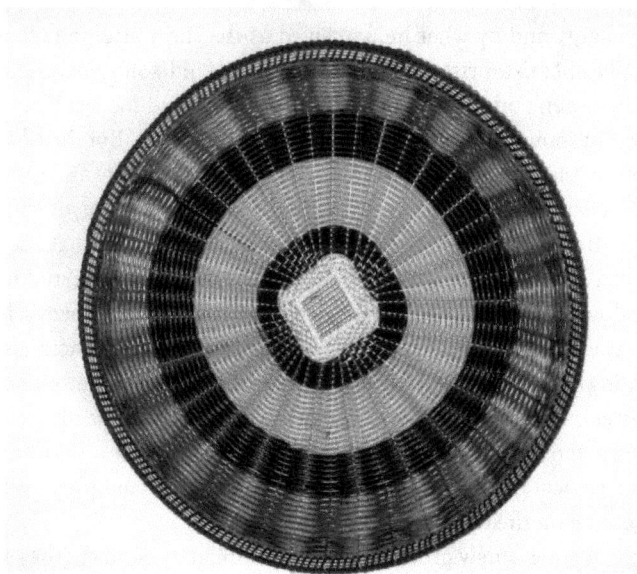

Figure 45. The prisoners from Loxicha eventually supplemented the standard basket type (a tall rectangle handy for carrying produce home from the market) with other shapes of baskets, such as colorful platters like this one.

practical than the basic tall rectangular shape for shopping in Mexican public markets, but quite attractive (figure 45). But each interested outsider had limited space in his or her suitcase for such items, and political liberals from abroad willing to buy these plastic (and thus less literally traditional) baskets constituted a limited constituency. Their enthusiasm melted away as they encountered fresh novelties, and progressively fewer of the prisoners' baskets sold.

The exhausting routine of camping on the square wore on these protesters, and in 2002 the state government sidetracked their remnants into a grubby but sizable apartment a few blocks north of the square. That July, I interviewed one of the few leaders not in prison, Desiderio Almarez. He outlined the development of the group's tourist wares: first the shopping baskets, then a round platter type and other new shapes (unusual in the context of prison-made nylon weavings), then paintings. He seemed discouraged by the waning of the prisoners' families' collective energy and by what he perceived as the short attention span of politically liberal tourists. No baskets of any kind sold anymore now that they weren't on the square; I may have purchased the last black one (as a way of showing my appreciation for the interview). But the Loxicha Zapotec, while "normal" victims of the incessant unrest of rural Oaxaca, had been on to something: they realized that the opinions of tourists could matter. By camping on the square and making sure that tourists didn't just see them but also interacted with them, they fostered international awareness of their plight and thus inhibited the heavy hand that Oaxaca's upper class reflexively employs to support caciques. By generating publicity through their presence on the square, gathering signatures on their petition, and selling attractive but politically charged souvenirs, they explored the concept that imperiling the continuity of tourists' critical contributions to the local economy could be a way to put pressure on the upper class.

Later in 2002, a new group arrived to camp on the square. They were wives and families of prisoners recently swept up in rural Las Huertas, Teojomulco. In one more episode in the tragic march of similar ones, desperate poverty yielded fatal punctuation to a long-simmering agrarian dispute with another village—the massacre of twenty-six men. That dispute may also have had an ethnic element. The residents of Santiago Xochitepec (a Zapotec community) claim that men from Las Huertas (mestizos) did the killing. However, citizens of Las Huertas blame local paramilitaries, which certainly exist and would have been more likely to have owned the powerful semiautomatic weapons employed. The state government, in a characteristically swift and crude response, sent armed forces to arrest many men from Las Huertas, with the overt goal of capturing the actual villains, but a broader purpose of keeping the violence from growing into a local war. This typically draconian strategy stripped Las Huertas of its leaders and left many families without income. Wives and families moved to Oaxaca, setting up camp in the exact area on the square that the authorities had just convinced the group from Loxicha to vacate. The new arrivals set out bedding, built campfires, posted numerous hand-lettered protest signs, and began begging for financial support from tourists. They also sold produce from home, charged tourists a few pesos to use their portable toilet, and, after a few months, had their own men's colorful plastic baskets from prison to sell.

During the 2002 Guelaguetza, the protest leaders from Las Huertas, Teojomulco, acting in concert with a variety of small antigovernment political groups, directly addressed the discrepancy between their sad situation and the happy—if largely fictive—prosperity of Indian life as willfully portrayed in the festival. The night before the first Monday of the festival, when the dance delegations paraded through the streets of the old city, the protesters paraded too. Signs they carried asserted: "¡La Guelaguetza Osculta Nuestra Miseria y Explotacion!" (The Guelaguetza masks our misery and exploitation!), "¡La Guelaguetza es hoy el exhibicionismo del gobernador!" (Today's Guelaguetza is the governor's show!), and "¡Baja con los grupos de poder nos usen como carne de cañon!" (Down with the groups in power that use us as cannon fodder!) The next day, protesters blocked intersections near the square, allowing cars through only after donations were solicited from and flyers handed to both motorists and pedestrians (obvious foreigners received an English-language version). The police quietly dispersed this serial blockade, but the point had again been dramatized: much (or most) of rural Oaxaca is in terrible shape. And while reasonably heedless teenagers make up most of the Guelaguetza's dance troupes, not all dancers are willing to be complicit in being caricatured as happy people possessing charming folklore. During the years that families from Loxicha lived on the square, dance ensembles (particularly central valley troupes presenting the Danza de la Pluma) would occasionally put on a show on their behalf, performing in the street bordering the encampment while flanked by protest banners (as in figure 3).

Why does the state government let group after group camp and protest in such a public spot? Perhaps this permission drains off some of the energy of the villagers' outrage at the mass arrests or at least dampens sympathy from the general populace. In any case, the downtown location provides a reliable rivulet of outsiders' money to support the bereft families.

These three episodes in which refugees from poorer parts of the state of Oaxaca were conspicuous on the city's central zócalo illustrate stages in the progressively more focused publicizing of their plights to tourists. The displaced Triqui were visible to tourists simply because everyone gravitates toward Oaxaca's city center, and poor people in the center (like most city residents) look to tourists for some income. The refugees from the Loxicha area addressed outsiders more directly through banners, basket sales, and even a petition suggesting that their situation and tourists' inclinations to visit Oaxaca might come to be linked. And the families from Las Huertas moved beyond passive appeals to accusation. The stage was set for the natural next step in this progression, the direct confrontation of tourism in both the rhetoric and the actions of the protests of 2006.

## Attempts to Bring Tourist Money to the Far Corners of Oaxaca

Did it make sense to sabotage the Guelaguetza as a violent capstone of what had been a largely peaceful protest? Were good-faith efforts to get some tourist money to those who needed it the most already under way? I examine in turn the immediate or potential financial contributions made (or not made) to the rural poor by private merchants, government programs and cooperatives, and the publicity attendant on participation in the Guelaguetza.

### Private Merchants

La Mano Mágica, the oldest and classiest of the dozens of Oaxaca's folk art stores, is owned by Mary Jane Gagnier de Mendoza (originally from Canada) and her husband, the well-known master weaver Arnulfo Mendoza. They met in Oaxaca in 1985 in a nightclub where he had rugs on display. In 1987 they married and founded the shop on a central street, Alcalá, which extends from the north side of the square to the Santo Domingo church and had just been transformed into a pedestrian corridor (this section of Alcalá remains the most prestigious few blocks in the state for tourist shopping). The Mendozas' original intent was simply to sell Arnulfo's weavings. When they decided to also sell other crafts, they were guided by a pair of principles that would become critical for Oaxaca's artisans. The first was that they would seek the intersection between craft and fine art (and thus sell items congruent in that way with Arnulfo's intricate silk weavings; see figure 23). Most of the Oaxaca crafts marketed to tourists now aim at that same intersection, but the work sold at La Mano Mágica is especially fine and, through the upscale character of the environment—uncrowded shelves, well-kept premises, consistent high quality of the goods, ability and willingness of the staff to talk about the culture and history of producing the crafts, and, in general, the hospitable rather than high-pressure sales environment— manages to make the relatively high prices palatable. Second, the Mendozas wanted to establish with the contributing artists and craftspersons relationships that gave those producers dignity. One gesture in that direction was encouraging the craftspersons to sign their work, which has since become the rule rather than the exception for local folk arts.

Many store managers exploit artisans mercilessly, and many others fall on a behavioral continuum between those rapacious capitalists and the comparatively benevolent owners of La Mano Mágica. Just a few well-established artisans do truly well. But the supply of crafts seems destined to always exceed demand. There is little incentive to employ artisans from outside the Central Valleys unless a region-specific product is notably striking. That might seem to describe many regions' huipiles, but women from nearby Mitla (and even some of the Triqui women living in the city of Oaxaca) have learned to copy the various local styles. The most authenticity-conscious buyers require assurances concerning sources of regional items, but customers who are both exacting and sophisticated in that way remain rare.

### Government Programs and Cooperatives

ARIPO (Artesanías y Industrias Populares del Estado de Oaxaca), the state organization that supports local arts and crafts, was founded in 1981 by government decree. It was recently renamed the IOA (Instituto Oaxaqueño de las Artesanias). Both names translate roughly as Oaxaca Institute for Crafts and Popular Arts. The institute is housed in a rambling structure about seven blocks north of the square. A dozen rooms surround a courtyard, with a majority of the rooms dedicated to sales, housing just one or two important crafts per room. The quality of the craftsmanship ranges from adequate to very good, and there is plenty of variety.

I interviewed David Salinas, then the head of social programs for the co-op, on July 23, 2002. He emphasized that his crew helps artisans gain business skills. They also gently guide aesthetic choices, trying to point craftspeople in directions that will increase sales while sacrificing authenticity only to the degree required to keep a craft commercially viable. They build on crafts already present in a municipality and do try to reach beyond the Central Valleys. The craftspersons they work with tend to be referred to them by ones whom they already know. Those who just walk in off the street are not allowed to sell in the ARIPO building but will receive some counseling. I found this to be a good enterprise in its intelligent and broad goals and, from the point of view of a customer, in its offering of a broader inventory than most (though this may simply have been a result of having enough room to continue to display old stock). But I was taken aback to learn that ARIPO was the major state enterprise serving in this way. In the half-dozen times I visited, I saw few customers there: due to the store's less-than-ideal location and unenergetic advertising, not much money seemed to change hands. It was, however, much more successful than the state-sponsored Mercado de Artesanias, a set of several dozen booths in a large building in an unfortunate location in the south part of town.

A much livelier enterprise is MARO (Mujeres Artesanías de las Regiones de Oaxaca, or Craftswomen of the Regions of Oaxaca), located in a prime tourism area on a street just a block east of the pedestrian corridor of Alcalá. The state government pays the rent for the sizable two-story premises. MARO has a great deal of stock, mostly mainstream in both quality and price, presenting an attractive variety allowed by sheer volume, and deliberately drawing on an exceptional geographic range within the state. The store is busy, and its success is based on its felicitous combination of broad offerings, good location, and the spirit of cooperation inherent in the business's name. Although the leader is mandated to be a woman, and although most of the visible employees are female, the title does exaggerate a bit. The requirement for participation is modest in terms of gender: each craft family must include at least one woman artisan. Very few artisan families in Oaxaca would be excluded on that basis. As an example, one room is full of rugs by a family from Teotitlán, a family of five weavers in which, as is typical, the father weaves the longest hours and makes the larger rugs. Nevertheless the combination of two concepts that appeal to many tourists concerned

with social justice—the co-op idea and female leadership, both strikingly unusual in Latin American context—draws many visitors to the
store, and the wide array of competently made crafts turns visits into
sales.

While MARO is not the only cooperative in the city of Oaxaca, it
is the oldest, largest, and most likely to survive. Of course, the public
markets are cooperatives in a way: individuals and families take home
most of the money that changes hands. All in all, craft sales in Oaxaca
city benefit organizers and owners of outlets the most, except in cases
of direct sales and in the few cooperatives. Nearly all the crafts sold in
the city are made in the Valles Centrales (with significant but still small
exceptions for some of those marketed in ARIPO and MARO). That
will probably continue to be the case, for several reasons. We need to
keep in mind that the crafts of the central valleys are not simply literal
replications of what has been made for a long time in given places—
they are transformed genres, made salable in accordance with careful
assessments of tourists' tastes. Communities elsewhere in the state have
lots of ground to make up not just in business skills and in publicity
and transportation costs but also in changing their inherited crafts to
become marketable—indeed, competitive with the oversupply of both
genres and quantities of items already available—without sacrificing the
economically valuable *appearance* of historical continuity.

*Publicizing Less-Accessible Locations in the State through the Guelaguetza*

One of the main reasons that communities in the state of Oaxaca send
dance troupes to participate in the Guelaguetza is to announce their
homes' attractions to tourists. Each act in the Guelaguetza does that in
two ways, through the display of local color in the dances and ceremonies
(and, if less obviously, making a more general claim that the act models
the character of their home: it's a peaceful, comfortable, fun place to
go), but also in the speech with which most acts commence, describing
traditions in and other features of their home and exhorting audience
members to visit. The planners who select the troupes must balance the
reliable appeal of regular participants making solid contributions with
the economic needs of municipalities that are seldom represented but

wish to participate. This becomes a political matter of sharing potential wealth but is also a process of shaping aesthetics, of creating a series of spectacles that evoke pleasant memories and also offer piquant surprises in an equilibrium satisfying regular paying attendees.

Is the state, through those organizers, making a serious attempt to reach out to new and poorer areas? I tracked which towns were represented in the Guelaguetzas from 1995 through 2007 and discovered a mildly encouraging trend. Yes, the big cities that contribute reliable signature acts are represented every year. But I recorded some statistics from the 2005 census concerning each participating municipality—population, number of residents speaking an indigenous language, percentages reached by services such as potable water and sewage, number of schools, and so on—and found that poorer, less-developed regions were gradually better represented. In my calculations, I ignored the invariable participants (the cities of Oaxaca, Huautla de Jiménez, and Tuxtepec), added up the populations of the other places sponsoring troupes performing in a given year, and divided those totals by the number of troupes counted. The locations in 2007 (that is, for the first official Guelaguetza of the year, and neglecting the giants) had an aggregate population about two-thirds of the size of that from 1995, with much of the progressive change occurring by 2002. The newly participating communities often had more residents who spoke an Indian language, and were reached by fewer services such as potable water and sewers. Thus the Guelaguetza has been slowly but surely reshaped to better represent the less-populous (and less-affluent) regions of the state, though how effective that has been in drawing tourists to those areas cannot be measured easily.

### Things Fall Apart: The Summer and Fall of 2006

When the teachers' union (the Oaxaca branch of the National Educational Coordinating Committee: Comité Coordinador Nacional de Trabajadores, or CNTE) went on strike in the third week of May 2006, their demands included a salary increase, better school buildings, and increased subsidies for students' school supplies—pretty much what they ask for each year, and what they get some of after a week or so of negotiation. They also asked for an increase in the federally determined minimum wage for the state (in poorer states such as Oaxaca, the minimum wage is especially low, because the government believes it is cheaper to live in such states). The negotiations did not move in their quarter-of-a-century-old rhythm toward a settlement, instead leading to teachers and a much larger group of allies than usual occupying the zócalo and surrounding blocks, and setting up the largest encampment there in living memory. Many small and a few very large protest marches took place. Then, on June 14, Governor Ulises Ruíz Ortíz ordered a predawn attack on the encampment. The state police destroyed tents and other personal property and beat and teargassed the teachers and their allies, including women and children. But the campers fought back with rocks and bricks and pushed the police out of the downtown.

It is hard to know how this dispute could have been resolved through negotiations after this point was reached. The governor was behind many known deaths and "disappearances" and had attacked free expression by, among many other actions, trying to close the best paper in Oaxaca, *Noticias*. After successfully repulsing the police attack on the zócalo encampment, the protests began to emphasize getting the hated governor to step down (not without precedent in Oaxaca, but not easy). The various protesting groups coalesced as a new organization, the APPO (Asemblea de los Pueblos de Oaxaca, or Popular Assembly of the People of Oaxaca). The June 14 police attack also destroyed a radio station set up by the APPO. In reply—and inevitably in escalation—students at the Benito Juarez Autonomous University of Oaxaca took over the university's radio station. Government forces wrecked the station by pouring sulfuric acid on the equipment. Then, on August 1, women in the APPO took over the state television and radio stations. After three weeks, state forces shot up the transmission facilities. After this, the rebel forces took over various commercial radio stations for various amounts of time.

Why did groups of protesters vandalize the Guelaguetza auditorium that July? A visiting American who sympathized with the more radical protesters summarized one broadly held opinion: "If tourists continue to flock to Oaxaca, pumping millions of dollars into the hands of the government and business elites that dominate the economy, then the chances of bringing about real democracy and rule of law in Oaxaca are greatly lessened" (G. Russell 2007). I've heard repeatedly that the teachers in the APPO not only had nothing to do with wrecking the auditorium but also condemned the action. But their numerous and more radical allies acted out their own convictions concerning how to further their mutual aims. Bringing "real democracy" to Oaxaca is a remarkable goal, given the equivocal position of democracy even in much more progressive parts of Mexico. In any case, groups of protesters blocked renovations on the auditorium and, on the night before the Guelaguetza was scheduled to commence, burned parts of the stage, spray-painted slogans here and there, and wrecked offices and even bathrooms. The government canceled the Guelaguetza. How many paying customers would have attended, anyway, since nearly all tourists had left the city by this time?

The APPO and its allies' occupation of the city would end in late October. On October 27, Brad Will, an American journalist and documentary filmmaker with a habit of manning barricades and consequently getting beat up (in several countries), was one of three individuals shot to death by state government paramilitary forces (not a matter of speculation—he filmed his killer while being murdered). Mexican president Vicente Fox, who had been treating the troubles in Oaxaca as a local affair best ignored, finally got involved. He sent some seven thousand federal troops to break up the barricades, at the same time requiring the state government to cut back on its sponsorship of what had been a steady trickle of drive-by murders of protesters. The result was a more diffuse series of protests, with fewer beatings or disappearances of protesters, but less dramatic protest actions, which continue as of this writing.

### 2007: Two Guelaguetzas, Two Visions of Oaxaca

I commenced my last brief research trip before finishing this book in early July 2007. I arrived in Oaxaca by bus and took a cab to the square (this is the moment described in the preface). There was considerable foot traffic on the zócalo, though the moderate level of crowding made it feel more like May than like a little over a week before the Guelaguetza.

That is, there was not even a shadow of the expected seasonal surge in visitors, the festive crush that in normal years made the square so thick with people and with craft stands that by the time of the Guelaguetza I would be surprised that any movement was possible, that I could actually traverse the square in no more than thrice the time required in the off-season. There were several sales tables staffed by protesters, though they simply sat passively unless passersby engaged them in conversation or bought something. Their wares included pop music compilations made by the protesters and videos of protest marches, of police action during the violence of July 2006, and of the "People's Guelaguetza" held at the edge of town to substitute for the one canceled due to the rioting and vandalism of the Guelaguetza auditorium that year. The activists looked like the teachers and college students that they were. I saw posters and wall graffiti advertising this year's People's Guelaguetza, averred to take place the Monday before the official Guelaguetza, and at the same venue, the refurbished auditorium on the hill. Had some rapprochement taken place between state and protesters?

On Sunday evening, a wind band representing a dance delegation in town to perform in the People's Guelaguetza played on the square. I listened briefly, then walked a few blocks north to the church at Carmen Alto, where the delegations were assembling for a march through town just like the marches made each year by participants in the official Guelaguetza (which the protesters were derisively calling the "commercial Guelaguetza"). At Carmen Alto, I saw gigantes (often locally called *monos*) being raised up, their human inhabitants peeking out at navel level; girl dancers were laughing and putting on makeup, and all the dancers were practicing a few steps. One troupe intrigued me, two lines of Indian boys pantomiming a battle between Turks and Christians (figure 46). The man in charge of the boys, none of whom stood taller than around five feet two, was at least six feet tall, and mestizo in physiognomy; he was probably their teacher in a secondary school. I tried to talk with one of the boys. He spoke in a language I didn't recognize to another boy, who could speak Spanish confidently. They were from San Agustin Tlacotepec, which I learned later was a tiny town (less than a thousand residents counted in the 2005 census) in a remote mountainous area not on the way to anything else, suffering from an unemploy-

Figure 46. A group of young boys from the small mountain town of San Agustin Tlacotepec, rehearsing a dance portraying a battle between Turks and Christians, at the staging ground for a parade the evening before the People's Guelaguetza (the church at Carmen Alto, just a few blocks north of the Oaxaca main square).

ment problem severe enough to be noted in the census: *most* men had to go to the United States to find work. But none of that was part of what the boy told me; he instead informed me that their municipal fiesta took place on August 27–29. He wanted tourists to visit—the same goal as that of participants in the regular Guelaguetza—and that celebration was their main attraction.

Later that evening, I ran into a different group of the young dancers I'd seen at Carmen Alto. They were from Pinotepa Nacional. Sleeping band members sprawled across a truck parked next to the square, while the girl dancers sat on benches and chattered a mile a minute. I asked if I could photograph them, which, like everything else going on, was highly amusing to them. They posed with teenaged drama, and I took a few pictures. With great ceremony, they chorused, "Thank you," then collapsed into giggles at their foray into English. I thought of them, I thought of the young boys waving papier-mâché swords at Carmen Alto, and I thought of the newspaper reports that the Guelaguetza Pop-

Figure 47. It was good that the main banner for the 2007 People's Guelaguetza could be erected anywhere, since the initial attempt to set up in the Guelaguetza Auditorium on the hill above Oaxaca was met with tear gas and riot police. Here the banner rises at the back of the Plaza de la Danza near downtown Oaxaca. Much of the morning wait for the festival to reconstitute itself in this fallback location (after the riot that disrupted the march of participants on the road up the hill) became a slow-moving serial photo opportunity as the delegations arrived one by one.

ular would not be allowed to take place on the hill. I shuddered to think of tear gas and truncheons.

The Monday morning of the People's Guelaguetza arrived. It was scheduled for 8 a.m., on the hill, though as late as Sunday evening, members of the APPO distributing literature on the zócalo had not been sure if it would take place: there were lots of police around, they dryly observed. I got up for a carefully timed walk to the base of the stairs that mount the hill. Having no desire to put myself in real physical danger, I hoped to arrive on time for the festival, but after any rioting would have taken place. Few others were walking in the direction that I was, and I couldn't see a crowd in the auditorium as I came into sight of it, though my view of parts of it was obscured by trees. At the base of the stairs, I encountered a police barricade, a solid wall of Indian-looking men behind a wall of large riot shields. I would not be walking up those stairs, evidently. I asked politely if the Guelaguetza Popular would be taking place somewhere other than on the hill, and the commander equally politely told me it would be at the Plaza de la Danza (just west of downtown, by the Soledad cathedral, a much-used public venue). I was allowed to take pictures of the soldiers—I was nervous, and my photos came out poorly—and then walked quickly down to the plaza. I need not have hurried, since the dancers would arrive gradually over the next four hours as a stage was slowly constructed from dozens of metal tables, a few large banners were hung (figure 47), and speech after speech was hoarsely shouted.

The atmosphere was simultaneously festive and wary. Plenty of families and friendship groups were there; it was like the free-seats audience at the official Guelaguetza. Vendors sold snacks, seat cushions with Guelaguetza emblems, sombreros, and ponchos and umbrellas to cope with the heavy rain, again just as at the official event. Then some firecrackers went off nearby, and what had been a relaxed, cheerful crowd panicked briefly. Some members of the crowd knew something that I would learn later, that the dance delegations and a few thousand members of the APPO had indeed marched a few hours earlier up a hill road toward the auditorium, where they encountered police and were dispersed with tear gas and with beatings that resulted in multiple hospitalizations. This explained the strain in the speech makers' voices as they cried over and over that the governor was an assassin, and the tears layered over the smiles on the faces of the girls from Pinotepa Nacional whose pictures I had taken the evening before. (I never did see the Turks and Christians from San Agustin Tlacotepec and silently commended the boys' guardian for taking them home when violence loomed.)

Once the People's Guelaguetza started, there were a few novelties, and rather more factors that surprised me through their normality, that is, how they remained the same as in the usual Guelaguetza. Most of the dances were familiar, and the ordering of the dance troupes was not surprising. The Chinas Oaxaqueñas led off as always. Huautla de Jiménez followed, again as usual, and the pineapple dancers and feather dancers were near the end, as had been the custom until a few years previous at the official Guelaguetza. Perhaps the Danza de la Pluma had originally been scheduled to go last. But heavy rain fell for much of the afternoon, and dancers were slipping. Danza de la Pluma men fell quite hard several times, and the dance was almost called off. But audience members suggested that a number of their chairs be cleared away to make enough room for the dance to continue there, and the men moved from the slippery platform to the pavement. This worked, and so the pineapple dancers, who I supposed had canceled their scheduled penultimate appearance owing to the dangerous conditions, returned to dance before all of us went home, soaked.

What was striking about this People's Guelaguetza? There were political speeches between the acts by APPO leaders, and sometimes also by the leaders of the dance delegations, so that the event lasted about four and one-half hours, over an hour longer than the norm for the official event. The order of troupes, although conventional as far as the aforementioned framing acts went, was organized geographically rather than for aesthetic purposes within the frame: the groups from a given region were in abutting time slots, perhaps to assert regional solidarity. There was no Diosa Centeotl parallel to the corn goddess of the official Guelaguetza; *all* Oaxacan women were beautiful, we were told by a male speaker, at which point a female speaker corrected him: "They're beautiful *and strong.*" The state band wasn't present, so the wind band from nearby Zaachila was pressed into service as the default ensemble, the one playing whenever a troupe hadn't brought their own musicians. There was no ramp on which dancers could take their special offerings to reserved special seats; there were no such seats. And there was no entrance fee, we were reminded numerous times.

"This is Oaxaca!" speakers yelled vehemently many times—the protesters and the state agreed that this indigenous festival (in some form) symbolized the essence of Oaxacan identity. The overall impression we were asked to carry away was that this was a much more egalitarian affair, since the seating was all first come, first served, and no tickets were sold. I did wonder where the financing came from: transportation, lodging, and food can't be conjured out of thin air.[1] And the speeches weren't just interminable; they centered on extraordinarily repetitive series of shouted protest slogans that the crowd often reinforced, shouts not particularly engaging for outsiders more interested in beautiful display than tempestuous politics.

I attended the first of the official Guelaguetzas on the following Monday. It had been a tense week in the city. Many signs posted each day in the square (and ripped down each night by government workers) stated

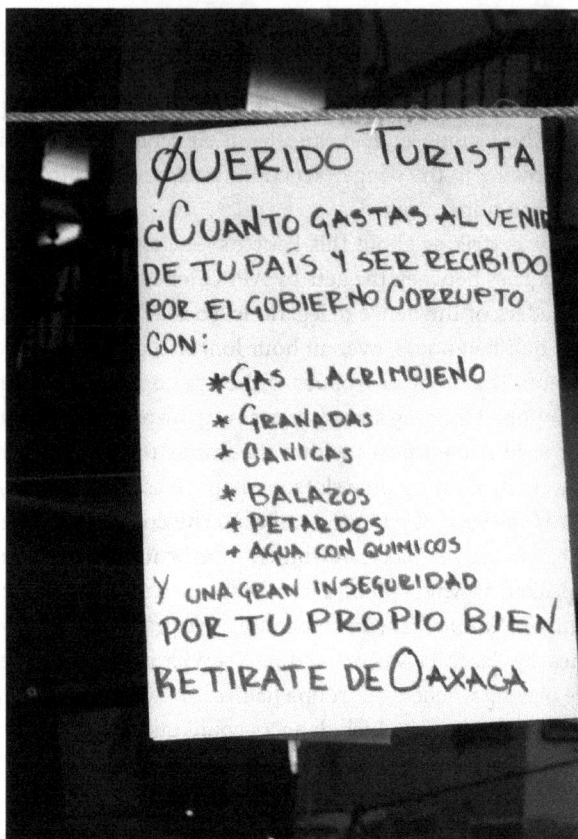

Figure 48. Signs hung during the week before the official Guelaguetza tried to steer tourists away from the event and stated their case in continually more aggressive terms. The police tore the signs down periodically; they quickly popped up again just as reliably. This one reads: "Dear Tourist, how much did you spend to come from your country and be greeted by a corrupt government with tear gas, hand grenades, grapeshot [or shrapnel], bullets, small bombs, water with chemicals [shot from water cannons], and a deep insecurity? For your own good, get out of Oaxaca."

that the "commercial" Guelaguetza would be stopped and that tourists should go home "for their own good" (figure 48). Merchants on the square had to display signs stating that they agreed with the APPO to be allowed to set up, and other signs warned (in vain) against patronizing rogue merchants. I photographed one affiliated hot dog vendor's stand bearing a common sign, a picture of a Danza de la Pluma performer in

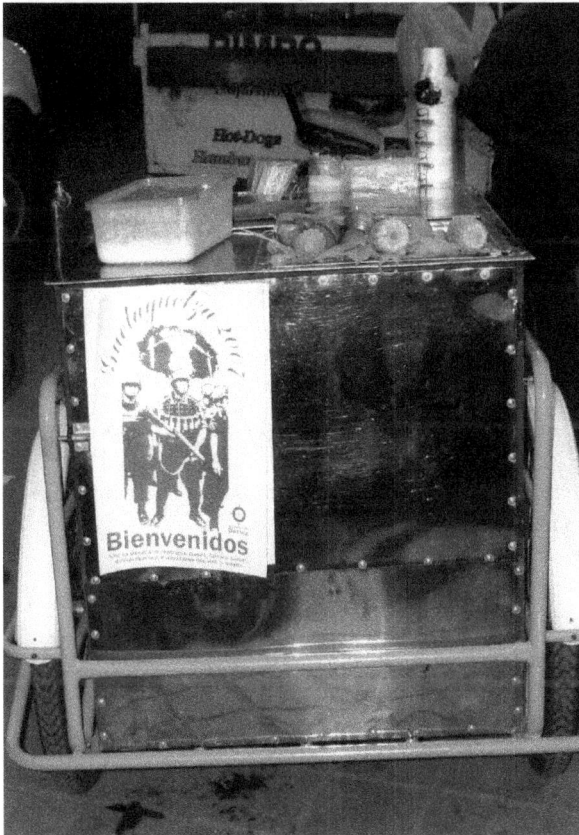

Figure 49. On the square, only vendors willing to declare they agreed with the protesters were allowed to set up unmolested. This hot dog vendor may or may not have felt aligned with the sentiments of this rather clever sign. "Welcome!" appears in large print, under which, in smaller print, follows a list of terrible developments in the state. In a sly parallel, the fact that the feather dancers are holding machine guns dawns on the viewer slowly, since the depiction of the weapons is stylized.

a characteristic pose, but carrying a machine gun, with clever words attached: "Guelaguetza 2007. Bienvenidos" (figure 49). These first words were printed in large type, and the gun was sufficiently stylized that one might have to look twice to tell what it was. The text continued in smaller writing, only legible within a few feet: "Sólo in Oaxaca encontrarás: Gases, tortura, cárcel, despariciones, detenciones ilegales y muerte"

(Only in Oaxaca do you encounter tear gas, torture, jail, disappearances, illegal detention, and death).

The bandstand, instead of hosting innumerable concerts as in the past, was draped with a giant mesh like a spiderweb, bedecked with photos of imprisoned APPO leaders and other protesters, as well as other slogans. Here is a sample of those, with translations:

No habrá PAZ in Oaxaca si antes no hay JUSTICIA. El gobierno es quien altera el ORDEN.
(There will be no peace in Oaxaca unless justice arrives first. It was the government that changed the ways things were.)

¡Presos Politicos LIBERTAD! ¡¡Fuera Ulises de Oaxaca!! Oaxaca no es cuartel. APPO sec XXII.
(Free the political prisoners! Ulises, get out of Oaxaca! Oaxaca is not a barracks. APPO section XXII.)

Nada por la fuerza todo don la razón y el derecho.
(Nothing for force; everything for reason and rights.)

Si Ulises no se va la paz no llegará.
(If Ulises won't leave, peace won't arrive.)

Liberación a detenidos al pasado 16 de Julio.
(Freedom for the prisoners of this past July 16.)

In this atmosphere, should or could the "real" Guelaguetza take place? The APPO said no, the government said yes, and writers in the newspapers called for peace. The presence of thousands of troops in town decided the matter on the side of the authorities. The protesters settled for graffiti renewed each night (figures 50–51) and for a giant march, the route of which was published in the newspapers.

The official Guelaguetza took place without further incident. In fact, the strangest thing about it was how absolutely normal it was intended to seem. True, there were none of the usual prestigious visitors from elsewhere, but the governor and his minions presided grandly. And the

Figure 50. Spray-painted graffiti protesting the official Guelaguetza. The graffiti, like the protesters' signs, was regularly erased (that is, painted over) by the authorities and was just as regularly replaced within a day or so. This message declares that art of the people should be (exclusively) for the people.

seats were full, though the newspaper that he had tried to suppress, *Noticias*, had the gall to note that most of the paid seats had to be given away to state employees, who were then required to attend; the occasion had to look busy and happy for the television cameras. Last, and most strangely, there was no mention of unrest, of an alternative Guelaguetza having taken place the week before, of any kind of cloud in the sky. While the vision of Oaxaca presented by the People's Guelaguetza advocated an instant and complete leveling of society, the official Guelaguetza displayed the government of Oaxaca in official denial. That vision of Oaxaca, one of continuing extreme socioeconomic inequality, seemed as unrealistic as that of the teachers and their allies. The two versions of the Guelaguetza both posit that some essence of Oaxaca lies in the dances and music that the versions share, but both Guelaguetzas also constitute tragically simplistic rhetorical gestures.

Figure 51. This stenciled graffiti sign was reproduced in several locations in and near downtown Oaxaca during July 2007: "Long live the People's Guelaguetza! Boycott the Commercial [official] Guelaguetza!"

## Can Oaxaca Recover?

The enduring unrest (coupled with the drug-related violence centered in the North and the association of Mexico with the swine flu epidemic) continues to be harmful to tourism and thus to the economy and to the overall mood of the city as the first decade of the twenty-first century comes to a close. Visitors encounter the pervasive malaise on arrival through their dealings with the service sector, that is, with cab drivers, hotel clerks, and so on. Fewer patrons means less income, with complex and sad results starting with money and ending in behavior. Each hotel manager downtown or in the other main tourist areas of the city has to decide whether to compete for rare customers with lowered rates, to rely on elevated rates to balance the losses resulting from reduced occupancy, or simply to close. In one hotel near downtown that I had patronized before, room rates had doubled, although south of the square and out of the tourist area, rates remained stable and reasonable. Restaurant managers cut back on staff and sometimes shrank their menus.

And goodwill and integrity could be eroded by desperation. I visited a family-run juice stand in the Benito Juarez market that I'd been to for breakfast nearly every day that I was in town for many years, and was overcharged by the husband. I skipped a day—which they noticed—then came back and ordered from the wife, who returned to the customary price structure with an apologetic look while her husband looked off to the side, embarrassed. This sequence can stand for numerous small, uncomfortable encounters in which the thinning of tourist money leads to actions further discouraging tourism.

Sadly, while the protesters' aim in discouraging tourism is to force change in Oaxaca by hitting the rich in their pocketbooks, the poor have been hurt more, simply because they have little or no savings to draw on in hard times. Craftspersons who had been on the way up socioeconomically find their progress stymied. I visited Teotitlán del Valle and looked for Felipe Hernández and Isabel Gutierrez. I didn't encounter Felipe, but I heard he was feverishly trying to cultivate more international connections and so was in and out of town at unpredictable intervals. I did find Isabel at her usual station in the rug market in the town center. Her formerly solid command of English had slipped due to disuse. And she had little time to visit congenially, instead pressing hard for sales. She stocked fewer rugs than before and had replaced some of that stock with smaller, cheaper pieces and other inexpensive woven goods, because most of the few tourists now visiting Teotitlán were Mexicans, who, as a group, are less oriented toward ethnic goods. The remaining Mexican vacationers cared little about large, "authentic" craft items, instead purchasing, for example, placemats that are both inexpensive souvenirs and practical items for home use. Last, Isabel's apron symbolized the new reality: it was of the same quality and general appearance as ones worn by the poorest women selling vegetables in the public market, a considerable step down for her (compare figures 19 and 32).

In the city, the big stores survived, though even Mary Jane Gagnier de Mendoza of the prestigious La Mano Mágica told me that she sold nothing at all for months after the climax of the troubles in late 2006 and had to stop purchasing additional inventory after a while. "At least we own," she said to me. Indeed, all the small rented stores on the main pedestrian street of Alcalá were shuttered, including the one that had been occupied by Felipe Hernández and his partner. Both in surviving city stores and out in the craft villages, inventories were dusty—and a little bland. Less turnover had resulted in reduced opportunity to innovate, and worry seemed to have blighted creativity. At Descanso, the largest rug outlet in Teotitlán, I was told that business was down about 75 percent, and that was the best news I heard in that town. The items that were moving in both the city and the villages were small things that fit Mexican tourists' circumscribed inclinations and the few European tourists' limited suitcase space.

Mexican tourism to Oaxaca has recovered somewhat, and Europeans are slowly returning, but the critical tourist constituency of Americans has barely started to resume visiting. A State Department travel alert scheduled to hold at least through March 2008—an "alert" is less alarming than a "warning," but nevertheless serious—read in part as follows:

*Oaxaca City*—U.S. citizens traveling to Oaxaca City should be aware that from May to November 2006, protests in Oaxaca City became increasingly violent resulting in at least nine deaths. On October 27, 2006, a U.S. citizen was shot and killed in Oaxaca City as a result of the violence and disorder caused by ongoing civil unrest in the city. Although recent demonstrations have not been violent, many of the issues that were the basis for the protests remain unresolved. U.S. Citizens planning to travel to Oaxaca City should check on current conditions before beginning their travel.

One can get the latest warnings at http://travel.state.gov. The text of this alert was true as far as it went, but still misleading. Outside the roughly sixteen blocks marked off by barricades in the center of Oaxaca at the height of the problems, travelers never encountered more danger than they might in Detroit or Los Angeles or my home metropolis of New Orleans. The fatally shot American had deliberately injected himself into the most newsworthy and thus most dangerous possible location. In fact, several Oaxacans whose offices front on the square told me that they went to work every day even during the worst of the confrontation, that both protesters and soldiers politely stepped aside for them to enter their workplaces. But it has been hard for Americans reading the news to differentiate between what actually was and is a highly focused confrontation and widespread lawless chaos; most potential tourists find other destinations.

An update of the State Department warning on April 14, 2008, was much longer. It contained the text cited earlier, but now following a half-dozen other paragraphs describing narcotics-related violence concentrated in the North near the U.S. border. Indeed, as the immediacy of the city of Oaxaca's own violence has begun to fade, the similarly discouraging general news about narcotics-related deaths in Mexico has risen. All this misery stems ultimately from poverty; none of it will encourage foreign tourism. Even more recent updates continue to shift emphasis to the north through progressively longer and more detailed warnings about violence between the drug cartels and the army, but Oaxaca's violence of 2006 is still cited as of late 2009.

The Guelaguetza, the former anchor for tourism in Oaxaca, could easily remain a focus for keeping tourists away and thus for keeping the city and state economies depressed. All that the protesters would have to do to ensure this would be to try to hold the People's Guelaguetza on the hill each year, just as was attempted during my visit in 2007. The governor would say no, the delegations would march anyway, and tear gas and billy clubs would be deployed just as in 2007 and shown on the news. The conflict could look fresh and violent as long as it recurred annually. That hasn't happened; I read that the 2008 People's Guelaguetza took place peacefully at a university soccer field on the outskirts of the city, and I learned that the 2009 one had been in the same place. Taken alone, this relocation suggests that while the protest will likely remain current, it has settled into a less-violent pattern, and various populations of tourists might well continue to slowly drift back to the city. However, there is no guarantee that the protesters will not return to their earlier, more confrontational actions. The 2009 strategy may prove to be a representative compromise. The People's Guelaguetza itself was indeed nonconfrontational in that there was no attempt to hold it on the hill. However, the protesters once again called for a boycott of the official Guelaguetza. To move the boycott beyond rhetoric, they scheduled the People's Guelaguetza against the first official one and energetically advertised theirs as a free and morally superior alternative to the commercial event on the hill.

Many factors echoed the settings of the previous years' multiple Guelaguetzas. First, in addition to the official and People's Guelaguetzas, nearby central valley communities held their own smaller alternative festivals, as always; this year the satellite events were in Culiapam de Guerrero, Zaachila, San Antonino Castillo Velasco, Ocotlan, Mitla, Ejutla de Crespo, Villa de Etla, and Miahuatlán de Porfirio Diaz (Chavela Rivas 2009). These are all towns that have sent troupes to one or the other big Guelaguetza over time; their forms of the festival are parallel efforts to attract tourists, with the smaller towns offering less crowded and stressful chances to see many of the same dances as in the main Guelaguetzas. There were the usual club mini-Guelaguetzas in the city of Oaxaca as described in chapter 3, and even a small Guelaguetza in which all participants were young people with Down syndrome. Second, there was a *planton* (protest encampment) on the zócalo for some forty-five days as the festival weeks approached. This time, it wasn't made of families of men imprisoned following violence resulting from agrarian conflicts in Oaxaca's rural municipalities, as in the years of the Loxicha and later Teojomulco camps. It was instead a group of teachers and APPO members advertising the state's dismal general politics, grabbing the special opportunity to publicize these problems in the time of the Guelaguetzas. I should note also that the villagers of Teojomulco had intended to be heard from during this fortnight of festival. Their crippling agrarian dispute with a neighboring municipality continued, the same dispute that in 2002 had resulted in violence, arrests, an encampment on the square, and a protest parade replete with anti-Guelaguetza posters—an explicitly unhappy parade mingling with the bevy of adamantly cheerful parades of dance troupes. Something similar to that protest parade but larger and much more disruptive seems to have been planned for 2009, but the fifteen buses of disaffected citizens headed from Teojomulco to Oaxaca City were stopped by state riot police well outside town, and the buses' tires (and spares) all flattened (Ruiz Jaimes 2009).

The focus for conflict in 2009 shifted to those customary parades of dancers on the evening before the Guelaguetza, parades offering audiences a taste of the color and movement and good cheer that would be displayed in full flower the next day. The troupes to perform at the

People's Guelaguetza paraded through the old city in much the same way as those scheduled for the official Guelaguetza, and with the same destination, the central square. Just as during my visit in 2007, so political protesters and craft vendors who were explicitly affiliated with the protesters had set up booths all over the zócalo. The intent of the organizers of the People's Guelaguetza seems to have been to have the two sets of parades appear indistinguishable in quality and style as a part of a general argument that the simultaneous festivals would be aesthetically the same; there would be no particular reason to pay fifty dollars a head to sit close to the dancers at the government-sponsored event. And when the various groups of dancers reached the square, those affiliated with the People's Guelaguetza would receive a warm welcome, and those belonging to the official event would not. This prospect offended the authorities to the point that they dispatched a phalanx of state police in riot gear to the square to eject the agitators and allied vendors. Most left peacefully, but enough resisted to ensure a dramatic and newsworthy *trifulca* (ruckus). One Triqui woman who declined to leave saw her wares kicked around by policewomen. A mask vendor attempted to help the Triqui woman. The police tried to shove him into a patrol car, and the crowd—including some tourists—pitched in to help him not be arrested. Outraged hearsay has it that a pregnant woman was kicked in the stomach by a policeman; perhaps four people were injured enough to seek medical attention.

As riots go, this was small potatoes. It served the short-term purpose of the state: to assert its authority and to dampen the celebratory intent of the "wrong" dance troupes' arrival on the square. But this suited the protesters even more, since all residents of Oaxaca who happened to be on the square, and all tourists present, and all who later read newspaper accounts of the "trifulca" saw once again that the official Guelaguetza is sponsored by a heavy-handed state government, a government that substitutes crude force for dialogue, thus squandering moral authority. The coverage in *Noticias* of the pair of Guelaguetzas and of the disturbance the night before was clever.[2] The riot was described not in the regular news section of the paper but in the crime section, was recounted deadpan, and was accompanied by a photograph of a line of dozens of policemen bearing their enormous plastic shields, an intimidating line apparently positioned to protect a restaurant fronting on the square (Vasquez 2009).

The next day, the front page of *Noticias* presented sparkling praise of the official Guelaguetza, as it does every year on that Monday, and the People's Guelaguetza received absolutely parallel treatment on the last page of that section. I mentioned earlier that the 2007 People's Guelaguetza was an hour longer than the three hours and change of the official event. In 2009 the People's Guelaguetza, now swollen to some twenty dance troupes (and lots of speech makers), took more than seven hours from start to finish. It surrounded the partially concurrent official Guelaguetza in time, both starting earlier and continuing long after. Of course, there was just one People's Guelaguetza, and four official ones (two per Monday); publicity of the government's version continued after that of the protesters faded. The official Guelaguetza was again visited by a few prominent guests and seemed financially sound.

How much of the former, more rosy image of indigenous southern Mexico will be left to attract ethnicity-oriented tourists if and when conflict ebbs sufficiently for foreigners to not feel significantly threatened? The colonial city will still be there, of course. Nevertheless potential visitors from outside of Mexico who pay attention to the news will arrive with a more nuanced—and less comfortable—understanding of Oaxaca. They will know that the state of Oaxaca, like its southern neighbor, Chiapas, is not just a pastoral idyll replete with living nostalgic images but also a culturally complex locale in which the attractive distinctiveness of Indian life owes its vividness and longevity at least in part to long-term oppression. On the other hand, despite the great degree to which the young tourist industry flourishes atop historical exploitation, making crafts can and often is done in a way that "selling tradition" doesn't ruin it—whatever that tradition really is. And the modest income from marketing the actually new but plausibly old crafts really does protect aspects of traditional life, especially the integrity of family and community, particularly in the central valleys. Last, visitors may still have a choice of Guelaguetzas to attend, festivals visually and sonically almost identical, but politically very different.

What if the crafts and festivals now supported by tourism do be-come casualties of the current economic blight? Even if that happened, the modern traditional crafts and practices *not* supported by tourists at this time, the ones sampled in chapter 4, would not disappear. There is a remote chance that this array of traditions, unaffected because they are largely ignored by visitors, might form the basis for a new tourist-defined "authenticity" as time passed and, politics allowing, as tourism revived in force. Then these crafts and practices might be preserved in museum fashion when they were no longer practical in vivo, just as hap-pened to the current tourist-oriented crafts, while yet other traditions arise among working people, traditions that respond to the changing conditions of the present.

Thus the vigorous nontourist traditions offer some vague hope for a kind of cyclical continuity. However, some craftsmen working in the earlier tourist crafts are finding enough income to press on through Internet sales. Others, driven by recent events to other professions by the shrinkage of tourist-based income, do not find this change psycho-logically devastating (apart from the distress accompanying reduced in-comes), perhaps partly because of the strength of new traditional crafts outside the tourist sphere. If their customers return, they may simply—and, in emotional terms, seamlessly—return to making tourist-oriented crafts, perhaps with fresh ideas. The problem that won't go away in the near future is this: the unsettled conditions in Oaxaca and in Mexico in general discourage American tourists, the staunchest purchasers of crafts. At the same time, the fact that the worst unrest in the country is in the north seems to be funneling Mexican vacationers to the south. They are attending the Guelaguetzas—both types, in similarly large numbers; Mexican politics does not shock or confuse Mexicans—and refilling hotels and restaurants.

As do the Zapatistas in Chiapas, the large and diverse body of protest-ers in Oaxaca desires rapid and comprehensive improvements. Which combination of paths to sorely needed change will prove most valu-able is impossible to predict. Ethnic tourism, focusing on sales of crafts and attendance at festivals, will continue to offer the best support for gradual change throughout Indian Mexico, but whether that change will continue to be considered far too gradual by enough residents that they scotch this factor as they did in Oaxaca in 2006 and 2007 is hard to predict. Will a useful compromise be found?

A reporter for *Noticias* speculated that a surge in tourism in Chiapas a few years after the Zapatistas had briefly occupied San Cristóbal did not occur in spite of the political troubles but rather consisted of adventurous Europeans who found the armed political standoff in Chiapas intriguing. He called this "guerrilla tourism" (Pasaran Jarquin 1998). However, Oaxaca could not expect a substantial boom in tourism based on that factor, since Europeans constitute a much smaller fraction of the tourist populace in Oaxaca than in Chiapas. Other types of tourism that may or may not overlap with aspects of ethnic tourism retain a modest but real appeal. There is tourism by medical personnel, in which, for example, teams of dentists from the United States conduct clinics in remote villages for a week or so, then relax in the city of Oaxaca for a few days. There is also tourism connected with pilgrimages (notably by Mexican travelers to Juquila), tourism flanking Protestant missionary activity, and ecotourism (in all cases with the same basic schedule as tourism by medical personnel). I have chatted with representatives of all these groups on the square. I would expect that their reasons for coming to southern Mexico would leave them relatively unaffected by the current political problems. In general, niche or special-interest tourists such as these are relatively well informed and thus less likely to be spooked by U.S. government warnings painted with unsuitably broad brushes.[3] And such tourists would go home able to narrate more accurate pictures of what Oaxaca is like now than those suggested by the crude warnings cited by the State Department, and perhaps allay the caution of other potential visitors from the United States. The best hope for a resurgence of international tourism and a return to relative prosperity for the craft villages may lie simply in the passage of time. The year 2006 was certainly not the first time that insurgents have occupied the center of Oaxaca, and visitors have gradually come back before.

We are left with conflicting narratives asserting what the Guelaguetza is about, and thus how we are to understand and enjoy Indian culture in Oaxaca. Those narratives are tied to larger questions concerning how to make Oaxaca more prosperous and more economically just. My tour of the city zócalo on arriving in Oaxaca for what turned out to be competing Guelaguetzas highlighted those narratives in a troubling way. On earlier visits, I was allowed by the physical setup of the square to take turns being socially aware (while briefly interacting—at my option and only when I wished—with the serial refugee encampments) and being a more detached ethnic tourist (whether harboring scholarly intent or not). Since the troubles of 2006, the lack of a demarcation on the square between protesters and crafts salespersons, and thus between disquieting politics and vacation fantasies, pushed all tourists who visit the city center into thinking in a more integrated way about Oaxaca, into considering the interdependence of its charm with its poverty and insalubrious politics.

I am confident that in time, either the energy of the disaffected Oaxacans will wane, or this especially confrontational state government will ease back to former, more practical levels of oppression, or both. And perhaps the publicity of narco-violence will fade, or the actual violence might lessen, and fewer potential visitors will be discouraged by that complex of factors. In any case, the old Oaxaca still thrives away from the city center and in the surrounding villages. Up a street toward the church Carmen Alto where I saw dance troupes preparing for the People's Guelaguetza, there is little evidence of political activity. During any festival, here we find snack stands, craft booths, and a couple of tiro al blanco shooting galleries blaring out rancheras and corridos when the targets are hit. And in the villages, while many craftspersons have had to go north and become mojados to earn a living (see Barbash and Ragan 2007), others still weave and carve and throw pots, waiting for their dreams of economic betterment to be fulfilled as part of outsiders' travels in search of exotic, romantic nostalgia, that is, waiting for ethnic tourists to return in force.

# Notes

## 1. Introductory Case Study

1. To cite a more recent example: some twenty-five Indians in one hamlet were killed between 1965 and 1985 because they tried to occupy land granted to them by presidential decree in 1965—but which ranchers with hired gunmen declined to cede (P. Russell 1995, 11).

2. This has been studied especially intensively in the hamlet of Zinacantan (see the bibliography in Vogt 1994).

3. "Los antepasados cuidan la sociedad y enseñan como vivir a través de los sueños. Son seres sobrenaturales como los santos." Morris has best summarized the position of the ancestors in Indian cosmology:

> The *Totil Me' il*, literally "Fathers-Mothers," also known as the Ancestors, reside in the mountains above each community and watch over the lives of their children. The Ancestors summon those with strong souls in their dreams to show them the proper and holy path of life and give them power over the jealous witches and demons that plague the night. People who ignore the Ancestors' teachings ignore the path that was laid down at the beginning of the world. Those with weak souls will grow ill.
>
> The Ancestors represent the first people who learned how to plant corn, praise their creator, and live as proper human beings. Like the saints, they are not anyone's direct ancestors but supernatural beings who guard the entire community. The Ancestors and the saints are members of a family who meet to discuss the state of the world. God has empowered them both to intercede on behalf of mankind. The saints are the more remote group, for they are the stars that wander across the distant sky. The Ancestors dwell in the nearby mountains and hear more clearly their children's pleas for health and knowledge. (1987, 153)

4. FONART is the Fondo Nacional para el Fomento de las Artesanias (National Foundation for the Encouragement of Folk Arts). A group with a related mission, INI, is the Instituto Nacional Indigenista (National Indian Institute).

5. This resembles how Peter T. Furst convinced the Huichol shaman and artist Ramón Medina Silva to convey Medina's inner vision of Huichol mythology (to Medina,

literal history) in the traditional medium of yarn paintings (Furst 1978, 26–27; Furst 1986, 179–80). The Huichol are a Mexican indigenous population of under twenty thousand living mainly in the northern sierra.

## 2. Crafts and Tourism in Oaxaca

1. Offering a rare glimpse at the earlier life of what would later swiftly evolve into this tourist-oriented craft, Herbert Corey of *National Geographic* magazine wrote about and offered photographs of weavings he saw during a visit to Oaxaca in 1927. He described Teotitlán as "where the serapes are made" by "both men and women," characterizing serapes as "gaudy blankets" (Corey 1927, 532, 511, 549). He portrayed his trip as a genuine adventure during which he passed through entertainingly dangerous situations—in Puebla, he suavely navigated riots—to reach a romantic idyll represented by Teotitlán's serape-weaving culture: "The Indian who wove them on a hand loom [in every household worked] in the cool shadow of the portico of his little hut, by the side of which, under the peach trees, a little stream tinkled in a stone-lined ditch" (549).

2. Why a yak? It's true that Tibet is far from Mexico, but copies of *National Geographic* are passed around the carving towns, allowing the craftspersons to supplement their fantasies with exotic reality, to explore more shapes, and to establish new mercantile niches.

## 3. Tradition and Tourism in Festival Life

1. The best concise description I have seen of the actual meaning of the Zapotec word comes from Mary Jane Gagnier de Mendoza: "Not to be confused with a folkloric dance festival in the city of Oaxaca, guelaguetza is best explained as a private, internal loan system whereby items of fixed value are given and received. For example, if you give two hundred tlayudas [very large corn tortillas] in guelaguetza for a neighbor's fiesta, you will get two hundred tlayudas back from that neighbor for your own fiesta. Each family maintains its 'savings and loans' ledger, writing down accounts of all guelaguetzas in detail—from the weight of a turkey to the quantity of tlayudas; the date of the guelaguetza, and who is was given by or received from. Many couples begin giving guelaguetzas years before they may need them, often saving for a son's wedding when the child is still in primary school" (2005, 32).

2. Also spelled Trique, roughly as often.

3. I extracted most statistics like these from the online *Enciclopedia de los municipios de México*, which in turn relies heavily on the 2005 national census. http://www.e-local.gob.mx/work/templates/enciclo/oaxaca.

4. In recent years, an evening performance has been added on both Mondays. Some of the dance troupes perform both morning and evening, others just once.

## 5. Things Fall Apart

1. I heard later that each Guelaguetza Popular was financed by contributions from the teachers, but I wonder how sustainable a strategy that will prove to be.

2. Concerning the Sunday disturbance, see http://www.noticias-oax.com.mx/flipping_book/oax/2009/07-jul/19-07-2009/seccion_b/pags.html, and turn the page several times until viewing page 9B of the newspaper. Both Guelaguetzas were described (with lovely photographs) the next day.

3. Gibson and Connell, at the beginning of a recent book about one sort of niche tourism, music tourism, explore the broad picture of recently burgeoning tourism that is highly targeted, for example, on history, parks, exotic biology, where certain books were written, film connections, art, crime, religion, sport, food and wine, battlefields, the pursuit of certain health benefits, et cetera, often with the purported focus hybridized with nostalgia (2005, 1–2). My father, Jack Goertzen, a retired soil chemist and agronomist, can stand for many of what might be called extreme niche tourists. As a member of the American Penstemon Society, he has ventured all over the world to witness nice stands of species within that plant genus thriving in the wild. The society's 2009 meeting will be held in northern Mexico. The members will pass through areas suffering from highly publicized drug-related violence, but as relatively knowledgeable niche tourists, they are not intimidated by the media's (and our State Department's) routine hyperbole.

# References

Acevedo Conde, María Luisa. 1997. "Historia de la Fiesta de los Lunes del Cerro." In *Historia del arte de Oaxaca*, ed. Margarita Dalton Palomo and Verónica Loera y Chávez C., 357–77.

Aguirre Beltran, Gonzalo. 1967/1979. *Regions of Refuge*. Repr. Washington, D.C.: Society for Applied Anthropology.

Amnesty International. 1986. *Mexico: Human Rights in Rural Areas; Exchange of Documents with the Mexican Government on Human Rights Violations in Oaxaca and Chiapas*. London: Amnesty International. Quoted at http://www.uscis.gov.

——. 1990. "Mexico: Reports of Human Rights Violations against Members of the Triqui Indigenous Group of Oaxaca." *AMR* (London) 41 (11): 1. Quoted at http://www.uscis.gov.

Barbash, Shepard (text), and Vicki Ragan (photographs). 2007. *Changing Dreams: A Generation of Oaxaca Woodcarvers*. Santa Fe: Museum of New Mexico Press.

——.1993. *Oaxacan Woodcarving: The Magic in the Trees*. San Francisco: Chronicle Books.

Berrin, Kathleen, ed. 1978. *Art of the Huichol Indians*. New York: Abrams.

Caballero, Ercily. 2002. "CEAMO, el apoyo de los migrantes oaxaqueños." *El Imparcial*, July 25, 6A.

Cancian, Frank. 1992. *The Decline of Community in Zinacantan: Economy, Public Life, and Social Stratification, 1960–1987*. Stanford, Calif.: Stanford University Press.

Chavela Rivas, Silvia. 2002. "Se espera derrama turística anual de $5 mil millones: Sedetur." *Noticias*, July 29, 9A.

——. 2009. "Habrá guelaguetzas simultáneas en pueblos de Valles Centrales." *Noticias*, July 15, 3A.

Chibnik, Michael. 2003. *Crafting Tradition: The Making and Marketing of Oaxacan Wood Carvings*. Austin: University of Texas Press.

Cohen, Erik. 1988. "Authenticity and Commoditization in Tourism." *Annals of Tourism Research* 15 (3): 371–86.

——. 2004. *Contemporary Tourism: Diversity and Change*. New York: Elsevier.

Collier, George A. 1975. *Fields of the Tzotzil: The Ecological Bases of Tradition in Highland Chiapas.* Austin: University of Texas Press.

Collier, George A., with Elizabeth Loery Quaratiello. 1994. *Basta! Land and the Zapatista Rebellion in Chiapas.* Oakland, Calif.: Institute for Food and Development Policy.

Corey, Herbert. 1927. "Among the Zapotecs of Mexico: A Visit to the Indians of Oaxaca, Home State of the Republic's Great Liberator, Juárez, and Its Most Famous Ruler, Diáz." *National Geographic Magazine* 15 (5): 501–53.

Dallal, Alberto. 1997. "Elementos míticos e históricos de la Danza de la Pluma." In *Historia del arte de Oaxaca,* ed. Margarita Dalton Palomo and Verónica Loera y Chávez C., 339–55.

Dalton Palomo, Margarita, and Verónica Loera y Chávez C., eds. 1997. *Historia del arte de Oaxaca.* Vol. 3, *Arte Contemporáneo.* Oaxaca, Mexico: Instituto Oaxaqueño de las Culturas.

Danly, Susan, ed. 2002. *Casa Mañana: The Morrow Collection of Mexican Popular Arts.* Albuquerque: University of New Mexico Press.

Eber, Christine. 1995. *Women and Alcohol in a Highland Town: Water of Hope, Water of Sorrow.* Austin: University of Texas Press.

Eber, Christine, and Christine Kovic, eds. 2003. *Women of Chiapas: Making History in Times of Struggle and Hope.* New York: Routledge.

Eber, Christine, and Brenda Rosenbaum. 1993. " 'That We May Serve beneath Your Hands and Feet': Women Weavers in Highland Chiapas, Mexico." In *Crafts in the World Market: The Impact of Global Exchange in Middle American Artisans,* ed. June Nash, 155–79. Albany: State University of New York Press.

Espina, Carolina. 2002. "Migrantes envían más dinero que los ingresos por turismo." *Noticias,* July 29, 7A.

Fábregas Puig, Andrés, and Carlos Román García. 1994. *Al fin del milenio: El rostro de la frontera sur.* Tuxtla Gutiérrez, Chiapas, Mexico: Gobierno del Estado de Chiapas y Instituto Chiapanéco de Cultura.

Forcey, John M. 1999. *The Colors of Casa Cruz: An Intimate Look at the Art and Skill of Fidel Cruz, Award Winning Weaver.* Oaxaca: Impresos Arbol de Vida.

Franck, Harry A., and Herbert C. Lanks. 1942. *The Pan American Highway: From the Rio Grande to the Canal Zone.* New York: D. Appleton–Century.

Furst, Peter T. 1978. "The Art of 'Being Huichol.' " In *Art of the Huichol Indians,* ed. Kathleen Berrin, 18–34. New York: Abrams.

———. 1996. "Introduction to Chapter 6" [Ramón Medina Silva, "How One Goes Be-
ing Huichol . . ."]. In *People of the Peyote: Huichol Indian History, Religion, and
Survival*, ed. Stacy Schaefer and Peter T. Furst, 169–85. Albuquerque: University of
New Mexico Press.

Gagnier de Mendoza, Mary Jane. 2005. *Oaxaca Celebration: Family, Food, and Fiestas
in Teotitlán*. Santa Fe: Museum of New Mexico Press.

García Canclini, Néstor. 1993. *Transforming Modernity: Popular Culture in Mexico*.
Trans. Lidia Lozano. Austin: University of Texas Press.

Garner, Bess Adams. 1937. *Mexico: Notes in the Margin*. Boston: Houghton Mifflin.

Gibson, Chris, and John Connell. 1995. *Music and Tourism: On the Road Again*. Buf-
falo: Channel View Publications.

Gilpatrick, Wallace. 1911. *The Man Who Likes Mexico*. New York: Century.

Glassie, Henry. 1993. *Turkish Traditional Art Today*. Bloomington: Indiana University
Press.

Goertzen, Chris. 2001. "Crafts, Tourism, and Traditional Life in Chiapas, Mexico: A
Tale Told by a Pillowcase." In *Selling the Indian: Commercialism and the Appro-
priation of American Indian Cultures*, ed. Diana Royer and Carter Meyer, 236–69.
Tucson: University of Arizona Press.

———. 2009. "Dance, Politics, and Cultural Tourism in Oaxaca's Guelaguetza." In
*Dancing across Borders: Danzas y Bailes Mexicanos*, ed. Olga Nájera-Ramírez,
Norma E. Cantú, and Brenda M. Romero, 293–317. Urbana: University of Illinois
Press.

Goolsby, William Berlin. 1936. *Guide to Mexico for the Motorist*. Mexico, D.F.: privately
published.

Graburn, Nelson H. H. 1989. "Tourism: The Sacred Journey." In *Hosts and Guests*, ed.
Valene Smith, 21–36. Oxford: Blackwell.

Greene, Graham. 1939. *Another Mexico*. New York: Viking.

*Guide: San Juan Chamula, Chiapas*. 1995. Tuxtla Gutiérrez, Chiapas, Mexico: Talleres
Gráficos del Estado.

Harris, Max. 2000. *Aztecs, Moors, and Christians: Festivals of Reconquest in Mexico
and Spain*. Austin: University of Texas Press.

Hulshof, Marije. 1991. *Zapotec Moves: Networks and Remittances of U.S.-Bound Migrants from Oaxaca, Mexico*. Amsterdam: Koninklijk Nederlands Aardrijkskundig
Genootschap.

Huxley, Aldous. 1925. *Along the Road*. London: Chatto and Windus.

Instituto Nacional de Estadistica Geografia e Informatica. 1991. *Estado de Oaxaca México: Guia turistica*. Aguascalientes: Instituto Nacional de Estadistica Geografia e Informatica.

Jackson, John Henry. 1937. *Mexican Interlude*. New York: Macmillan.

Jeter, James, and Paula Marie Juelke, with photographs by Michael Caden. 1978. *The Saltillo Sarape: An Exhibition Organized by the Santa Barbara Museum of Art*. Santa Barbara, Calif.: New World Arts.

Kirshenblatt-Gimblett, Barbara. 1998a. *Destination Culture: Tourism, Museums, and Heritage*. Berkeley: University of California Press.

———. 1998b. "Objects of Ethnography." In Kirshenblatt-Gimblett, *Destination Culture*, 17–78.

Kovic, Christine, and Christine Eber. 2003. "Introduction." In *Women of Chiapas: Making History in Times of Struggle and Hope*, ed. Christine Eber and Christine Kovic, 1–27. New York: Routledge.

Krippendorf, Jost. 1987. *The Holiday Makers: Understanding the Impact of Leisure and Travel*. Trans. Vera Andrassy. London: Heinemann.

MacCannell, Dean. 1975. *The Tourist: A New Theory of the Leisure Class*. New York: Schocken Books.

Marcus, Laura. n.d. *New Mexico Fiber Arts Trails: A Guide to Rural Fiber Arts Destinations*. Santa Fe: New Mexico Arts.

Mata Garcia, María Eugenia. 1996. "Economic Crisis and Rural Violence in Oaxaca, Mexico." Presentation at the Washington Office on Latin America, Washington, D.C., 26 September. Quoted at http://www.uscis.gov.

McKean, Philip F. 1989. "Towards a Theoretical Analysis of Tourism: Involution in Bali." *Hosts and Guests*, ed. Valene Smith, 124–44. Oxford: Blackwell.

M'Closkey, Kathy. 1994. "Marketing Multiple Myths: The Hidden History of Navajo Weaving." *Journal of the Southwest* 36 (3): 185–222.

Méndez Aquino, Alejandro. 1990. *Noche de rabanos: Tradiciones navideñas de Oaxaca*. Mexico City: Grupo Jaguar Impresiones.

Morris, Walter F., Jr. 1984. *A Millennium of Weaving in Chiapas: An Introduction to the Pellizzi Collection of Chiapas Textiles*. San Cristóbal, Chiapas, Mexico: Gobierno del Estado de Chiapas.

———. 1987. *Living Maya*. New York: Harry N. Abrams.

———. 1996. *Handmade Money: Latin American Artisans in the Marketplace*. Washington, D.C.: Organization of American States.

Mullin, Molly H. 2001. *Culture in the Marketplace: Gender, Art, and Value in the American Southwest*. Durham, N.C.: Duke University Press.

Murphy, Arthur D., and Alex Stepick. 1991. *Social Inequality in Oaxaca: A History of Resistance and Change*. Philadelphia: Temple University Press.

Nájera-Ramírez, Olga, Norma E. Cantú, and Brenda M. Romero, eds. 2009. *Dancing across Borders: Danzas y Bailes Mexicanos*. Urbana: University of Illinois Press.

Nash, June, ed. 1993. *Crafts in the World Market: The Impact of Global Exchange in Middle American Artisans*. Albany: State University of New York Press.

——. 2003. "Foreword: Activists, Poets, and Anthropologists in the Frontlines of Research." In *Women of Chiapas: Making History in Times of Struggle and Hope*, ed. Christine Eber and Christine Kovic, ix–xv. New York: Routledge.

Oettinger, Marion, Jr. 1997. *El alma del Pueblo: El arte popular de España y las Américas*. San Antonio, Tex.: San Antonio Museum of Art.

Pasaran Jarquin, Carlos. 1998. "Vertiginoso crecimiento presenta la industria turística in Chiapas." *Noticias*, June 22, second section A, 4.

Past, Ambar. 1980. *Bon: Tintes naturales*. Bilingual in Tzotzil and Spanish. San Cristóbal de las Casas, Mexico: Taller Leñateros.

Past, Ambar, and Juan Bañuelos. 1997. *Conjuros y ebriedades: Cantos de mujeres mayas*. San Cristóbal de las Casas, Mexico: Taller Leñateros.

Pelauzy, Antonia, with photographer Catalá Roca. 1978. *Spanish Folk Crafts*. Trans. Diorki. Barcelona: Editorial Blume.

Peterson, Anya. 1968. "An Acculturation Study of Some Dances of Oaxaca, Mexico." In *Researchers in Latin American Society*, by Anya Peterson and Ronald Royce, 37–79. Stanford, Calif.: Institute for the Study of Contemporary Culture.

Peterson, Anya, and Ronald Royce. 1968. *Researchers in Latin American Society*. Stanford, Calif.: Institute for the Study of Contemporary Culture.

*Programa Artesanal del dif Regional Zona II Altos*. n.d. Two-page photocopied typescript distributed in Casa de Artesanías, San Cristóbal de las Casas, Mexico, in 1997.

Ragland, Cathy. 2009. *Música Norteña: Mexican Migrants Creating a Nation between Nations*. Philadelphia: Temple University Press.

Rodrigo Alvarez, Luis. 1995. *Historia general de estado de Oaxaca*. Oaxaca: Carteles Editores.

Rothstein, Arden Aibel, and Anya Leah Rothstein. 2002. *Mexican Folk Art: From Oaxacan Artist Families*. Atglen, Pa.: Schiffer.

Royer, Diana, and Carter Meyer, eds. 2001. *Selling the Indian: Commercialism and the Appropriation of American Indian Cultures.* Tucson: University of Arizona Press.

Ruiz Jaimes, Elizabeth. 2009. "Impiden marcha de Teojomulco." *Noticias,* July 18, 16A.

Russell, Grahame. 2007. "Torture and Tourism in Oaxaca." *Upside Down World: Covering Activism and Politics in Latin America.* http://upsidedownworld.org/main/mexico-archives-79/595-torture-and-tourism-in-oaxaca.

Russell, Philip J. 1995. *The Chiapas Rebellion.* Austin, Tex.: Mexico Resource Center.

Schaefer, Stacy, and Peter T. Furst. 1996. *People of the Peyote: Huichol Indian History, Religion, and Survival.* Albuquerque: University of New Mexico Press.

Simonett, Helena. 2001. *Banda: Mexican Musical Life across Borders.* Middletown, Conn.: Wesleyan University Press.

Smith, Valene, ed. 1989. *Hosts and Guests.* Oxford: Blackwell.

Stanton, Andra Fischgrund. 1999. *Zapotec Weavers of Teotitlán.* Santa Fe: Museum of New Mexico Press.

Stephen, Lynn. 2002. *Zapata Lives! Histories and Cultural Politics in Southern Mexico.* Berkeley: University of California Press.

———. 2005. *Zapotec Women: Gender, Class, and Ethnicity in Globalized Oaxaca.* 2nd ed. Durham, N.C.: Duke University Press.

Stigberg, David. 1978. "*Jarocho, Tropical,* and 'Pop': Aspects of Musical Life in Veracruz, 1971–72." In *Eight Urban Musical Cultures: Tradition and Change,* ed. Bruno Nettl, 260–95. Urbana: University of Illinois Press.

Titon, Jeff Todd. 1999. " 'The Real Thing': Tourism, Authenticity, and Pilgrimage among the Old Regular Baptists at the 1997 Smithsonian Folklife Festival." *World of Music* 41 (3): 115–39.

Van Den Berghe, Pierre L. 1994. *The Quest for the Other: Ethnic Tourism in San Cristóbal, Mexico.* Seattle: University of Washington Press, 1994.

Vasquez, Yajaira. 2009. "Trifulca en el zócalo." *Noticias,* July 19, crime section B, 9.

Vogt, Evon Z. 1994. *Fieldwork among the Maya: Reflections on the Harvard Chiapas Project.* Albuquerque: University of New Mexico Press.

Whipperman, Bruce. 2000. *Oaxaca Handbook: Mountain Craft Regions, Archaeological Sites, and Coastal Resorts.* Emeryville, Calif.: Avalon Travel Publishing, Moon Travel Handbooks.

Wood, W. Warner. 2008. *Zapotec Weavers and the Global Ethnic Art Market.* Bloomington: Indiana University Press.

Wright, Dorothy. 1992. *The Complete Book of Baskets and Basketry.* 3rd ed. Newton Abbot, Devon, U.K.: David and Charles. (Orig. pub. 1983.)

Zug, Charles G., III. 1986. *Turners and Burners: The Folk Potters of North Carolina.*
    Chapel Hill: University of North Carolina Press.

# Index

"El Jarabe Tapatío," 93

embroidery, 22

encampment on Oaxaca city's zócalo, viii, xi, 102–3, 119, 140, 143–45, 151, 166, 171

encomiendas, 37

EPR (Ejército Popular Revolucionario), 140

Escher, M. C., 50, 54

Fernandez, Alejandro, 128–29

Fernandez, Vicente, 128–29

folkloric intensification. *See* intensification

FONART (Fondo Nacional para el Fomento de las Artesanías) (National Foundation for the Encouragement of Folk Arts), 20, 173

Forcella, Maddalena, 17–18

Forcey, John M., xii

Fox, Vicente, 152

Furst, Peter T., 173

Gagnier de Mendoza, Mary Jane, xii, 47, 63, 67, 146, 163, 174

gender roles, in traditional expressive culture, xii, 2, 13, 16–17, 27, 30–33, 58, 60–61, 125, 148–49

Gill, Craig, xiii

glass from Guadalajara, 22

Glassie, Henry, 8

Goertzen, Ellen, xiii, 47, 51

Goertzen, Jack, 175

Goertzen, Kate, xiii

Goertzen, Valerie, xiii

Gonzales, José, 47, 51, 55

Graburn, Nelson, 7–8

Greene, Graham, 7

Guadalajara, 125

Guatemala, 4, 38; refugees from, 26, 30

Guelaguetza, xi, xiii, 74–103, 115, 131, 135, 145, 154, 156–61, 165–71, 175; advertisement to tourists of dance troupes' homes' attractions, 82, 85, 149–50; alternative small Guelaguetzas, 95–96, 166; audience behavior, 78; auditorium vandalized, 135, 146, 151–52; authenticity committee, 97; budget, 75; dance outfits, 79, 88–89, 108; dance troupes, 75, 79–92, 145; dances, 79, 90; dances, ordering of, 86–87, 149–50, 156–57; general demography, 76; history, 76, 91; meaning and uses of term "Guelaguetza," 76, 78, 99–103, 174; music, 77–79, 90, 95–96, 130; participants in, 96–97; People's Guelaguetza (Guelaguetza Popular), 152–57, 161–62, 165–71, 175; performed on zócalo, x; political uses of, 101–3; souvenirs representing, vii, xii; stage and physical layout of grounds, 76–77; tourist support, 75, 77, 101; traditional fiesta, 90–96; transformation of, 100

Gutierrez, Isabel, 47, 50–51, 54–55, 57, 60, 108, 111, 163

Gutiérrez, Ismael, 45

Gutierrez Mendoza, Andrés, 137–39

Harvard Chiapas Project, 7

hats, 26, 130–31